DESIGN INVESTIGATIONS

AFTER ABUNDANCE

Edition Angewandte
Book Series of the University of Applied Arts Vienna
Edited by Gerald Bast, Rector

Universität für angewandte Kunst Wien
University of Applied Arts Vienna

AFTER ABUNDANCE

A Speculation

on
Climate Change
in the Alps

Edited by
Thomas Geisler

Anab Jain

Eine
S p e k u l a t i o n
zum
Klimawandel
in
den Alpen

Birkhäuser
Basel

Carving out a place for Austria and its art scene, while strengthening their presence on the international stage through active networking and dialogue, is a matter of great importance to me. Austrian art is widely admired for its outstanding quality: the aim is to make it accessible to a larger audience by increasing its international outreach.

The London Design Biennale was held for the first time in 2016. Created by mischer'traxler studio and curated by Thomas Geisler, the Austrian contribution "LeveL" was a great success. Further to this, the wonderfully poetic installation "LeveL – the fragile balance of utopia, a kinetic light installation" was also show-cased in Australia and Vienna.

Following on from the success of Austria's participation, the London Design Biennale invited the Federal Chancellery for a second time. From 4 to 23 September 2018, Austria had the opportunity to be involved in the current design discourse at Somerset House. Appearing in London was the ideal opportunity for Austria to present itself within the international frame-work of a biennial, as already happens with art and architecture in Venice, for instance.

Under the general theme of *Emo-tional States,* curator Thomas Geisler chose *After Abundance,* an exhibition designed by the students at the department of *Design Investigations* (Industrial Design 2), at the University of Applied Arts, led by Prof. Anab Jain, to take us from poetry, and an explo-ration of current social topics, through to drafting scenarios for the future. How do people shape their lives in the fast-paced 21st century? What positions and possible courses of action are relevant for future designers working with new materials and developing new technologies?

Austria's goal here is to build up a lasting international presence that will draw attention to the Austrian design scene, while creating the opportunity to examine fundamental questions about the future.

I would like to thank all of the coop-eration partners, the commissioner and the curator Thomas Geisler, Anab Jain, the students and everyone who was involved in the project, and also to offer my congrat-ulations on the successful design of the Austrian contribution.

GERNOT BLÜMEL
Federal Minister for the EU, Art, Culture and Media

Österreich und seine Kunst-szene durch intensive Vernetzung und Austausch international zu positionieren und zu stärken, ist mir ein grundlegendes Anliegen. Die hohe Qualität des österreichischen Kunstschaffens überzeugt und soll durch mehr Internationalität auch für ein größeres Publikum sichtbar sein.

2016 fand die London Design Biennale das erste Mal statt. Der erfolgreiche österreichische Beitrag „LeveL" wurde von mischer'traxler studio kreiert und von Thomas Geisler kuratiert. Die wunderbare poetische Installation „LeveL – the fragile balance of utopia, a kinetic light installation" konnte darüber hinaus auch in Australien und in Wien präsentiert werden.

Nach dieser äußerst erfolgreichen österreichischen Teilnahme wurde das Bundes-kanzleramt nun von der London Design Biennale zum zweiten Mal eingeladen. Von 4. bis 23. September 2018 gab es die großartige Möglichkeit, einen Beitrag zum aktuellen Design-diskurs im Somerset House zu zeigen. In London präsent zu sein war daher eine ideale Gelegenheit, einen österreichischen Beitrag im internationalen Rahmen einer Biennale zu leisten, wie dies bereits im Kunst- und Architektur-bereich z.B. in Venedig erfolgt.

Unter dem General-thema *Emotional States* führte uns der Kurator Thomas Geisler mit der von *Design Investigations* (Industrial Design 2) unter der Leitung von Anab Jain gestalteten Ausstellung *After Abundance* über die Poesie zur Auseinander-setzung mit gesellschaftlichen Themen unserer Zeit bis hin zum Entwerfen von Zukunftsszenarien. Wie sieht Lebensgestaltung im schnelllebigen 21. Jahrhundert aus, welche Haltungen und Handlungsmöglichkeiten sind für zukünftige Designerinnen und Designer relevant, die sich mit neuen Materialien aus-einandersetzen, neue Techno-logien entwickeln?

Die Republik Österreich engagiert sich hier, eine Konti-nuität internationaler Präsenz aufzubauen, die der heimischen Designszene Aufmerksamkeit entgegenbringt und ihr ermöglicht, sich mit grundsätzlichen Zukunfts-fragen auseinanderzusetzen.

Ich möchte mich bei allen Kooperationspartnerinnen und -partnern, beim Kommissär und Kurator Thomas Geisler, bei Anab Jain, bei den Studierenden und allen Beteiligten bedanken und zur erfolgreichen Gestaltung des österreichischen Beitrags gratulieren.

GERNOT BLÜMEL
Bundesminister für EU, Kunst, Kultur und Medien

Climate change is a reality. We can ignore, play down or even make a joke out of the fact that the climate is changing. None of this changes the reality of it, it just hinders the necessary reactions to this fact. Naturally enough, there are reasons for these avoidance strategies: the fear of the unknown, the fear of losing wealth and well-established profit perspectives, the fear of losing supposed control. Psychologists describe the phenomenon of how fears and repressing them lead to irrational, sometimes even self-damaging actions. Art—and here I include certain kinds of design—has always had the potential to enable people who engage with it to widen their horizons, to adopt new perspectives, to discover links that we could not make out without the aid of art. Anab Jain's design class's work on climate change is a good example of this. That this "Speculation on Climate Change in the Alps" was Austria's contribution to the London Design Biennale 2018 is not only a special distinction for the University of Applied Arts and for Anab Jain's students—the recognition given to the installation by visitors and reviewers is equally an acknowledgement of the University's emphasis: we understand "applied arts" as an expression of social responsibility, as a contribution to improving the world by means of the possibilities offered by art and design.

GERALD BAST
Rector of the University of
Applied Arts Vienna

Klimawandel ist eine Realität. Man kann die Tatsache, dass sich das Klima verändert, ignorieren, klein reden oder sogar lächerlich machen. Das alles ändert nichts an der Realität, es erschwert nur die notwendigen Reaktionen auf diese Tatsache. Natürlich gibt es Gründe für diese Vermeidungsstrategien: Angst vor dem Unbekannten, Angst vor dem Verlust von Wohlstand und bekannten Gewinnperspektiven, Angst vor dem Verlust vermeintlicher Kontrolle. Die Psychologie beschreibt das Phänomen, wie Ängste und deren Verdrängung zu irrationalen, bisweilen sogar selbstbeschädigenden Handlungen führen. Kunst – und da zähle ich bestimmte Arten von Design dazu – hatte schon immer das Potenzial, Menschen, die sich auf die Auseinandersetzung mit ihr einlassen, dazu zu befähigen, ihren Blickwinkel zu erweitern, neue Perspektiven einzunehmen, Verbindungen zu entdecken, die ohne die Kunst nicht wahrnehmbar waren. Die Auseinandersetzung der von Anab Jain geleiteten Design-Klasse mit dem Klimawandel ist ein gutes Beispiel dafür. Dass diese „Spekulation zum Klimawandel in den Alpen" Österreichs Beitrag auf der London Design Biennale 2018 in London war, bedeutet nicht nur eine besondere Auszeichnung für die Angewandte und für die Studierenden von Anab Jain – die fachliche Anerkennung, welche die Installation bei den Besucher*innen und Rezensent*innen erfahren hat, ist auch eine Bestätigung der inhaltlichen Ausrichtung der Universität für angewandte Kunst: Wir verstehen „angewandte Kunst" als Ausdruck gesellschaftlicher Verantwortung, als Beitrag zur Verbesserung der Welt mit den Wirkungsmöglichkeiten von Kunst und Design.

GERALD BAST
Rektor der Universität für angewandte Kunst Wien

EMOTIONAL DISRUPTION

Thomas Geisler

"What I hope we achieve at this conference is that we realise that we are facing an existential threat. This is the biggest crisis humanity has ever faced. First we have to realise this and then as fast as possible do something to stop the emissions and try to save what we can save."
Greta Thunberg

This galvanising wake-up call issued by the young Swede Greta Thunberg was heard not only by participants at the UN Climate Conference in Katowice in December 2018, but also went viral across the globe. By staging a school strike to demand that her home country fulfil their climate objectives, she triggered the international *Fridays for Future* movement among like-minded peers. The teenager reiterated her appeal for drastic changes in climate policy to high-ranking politicians and economic experts at the World Economic Forum in Davos in 2019: "I want you to feel the fear I do. Every day."[1]

And in view of the figures and forecasts presented in the run-up to and during the Katowice conference, any sensible person should indeed be afraid for the survival of Earth and of the effects of climate change.[2] Like joy, anxiety, love or hatred, fear too is a basal emotion and, according to evolutionary psychologists, is found in all civilisations. Primary affects thus enable a universally understood, non-verbal communication on the basis of emotions. Diagnosed with Asperger syndrome, it comes as some surprise that Thunberg uses the language of emotions in her messages, given that autistic people are generally said to have particular deficits in recognising and producing emotional signals such as gestures and facial expressions. Is it perhaps *we* who are reacting to climate change like autistic people? If even planetary warming leaves us cold, what does touch us?

Emotional States was the theme of the second London Design Biennale, which took place from 4 to 23 September 2018.

Around forty nations, regions and metropolises from six continents showcased their work at Somerset House on the Thames Embankment. In Space-embracing installations and exhibitions examined and negotiated current trends and conditions in design and associated artistic, creative and investigative disciplines. The aim of the show as a whole was to explore the role of design for a common future. Explaining the theme, the British curator and artistic director of the Biennale Christopher Turner noted: "Emotions are universal, with shared meanings that transcend borders. Thoughtful design and technology can create positive emotional experiences, facilitating new social possibilities by enabling connectivity and contact, and the forging of meaningful connections between people."[3]

Taking a self-critical look at the discipline of design, in their brief the organisers drew attention to the historical and contemporary fact that with every problem that designers seem to solve, more are created. Which is why we should not necessarily strive for design solutions in the technical or material, but rather in the immaterial or transcendent. Taking this as a starting point, this could lead to the following questions for elaborating entries: How can design evoke, visualise, communicate and perhaps even manipulate emotions? How can designers help to strengthen citizen and community engagement by encouraging positive feelings, promoting and supporting well-being? Conversely, how can design provoke and address negative effects, such as anger and stress? What are the possible consequences of creating robots that are emotional machines? How can we create emotionally durable designs that increase sustainability and reduce the impact of consumption and waste?[4]

After Abundance, the Austrian entry to the London Design Biennale 2018, focused on the importance of design against a background of increasingly scarce resources, predatory exploitation of nature, extreme climate and weather situations, and other precarious developments caused by climate change that we are seeing both globally and in Austria. The widespread emotional state to which this leads, both among those involved in the project and the public, between fear, panic, perplexity or helplessness, was intended to give rise to a productive, confident and heartening awareness. An optimistic approach that emancipates those who react to these complex issues and challenges with indifference or denial, constructively galvanising them into action.

As Austrians, we are particularly inclined to see ourselves as living on an "island of the blessed". One of the wealthiest countries in the EU, not only does our economically privileged situation blind us to the fate of those less fortunate[5], so does the country's Alpine location at the heart of the continent. Sea level rise caused by climate change and tropical storms are no cause for immediate concern, and drought seems inconceivable when there are plentiful water resources from mountain springs to reassure us. Nevertheless, the wide range of different views to be observed in this relatively small territory between urban, rural and mountain populations is striking. Just imagine a hot summer's day in Vienna—one of those "dog days"—or in the Salzkammergut, a summer holiday destination for many town-dwellers. Climate change sceptics see this as a centuries-old tradition or as evidence of social improvement: what was once a privilege reserved for the nobility and the rich middle classes is now democratically available to (almost) anyone—thanks to universal mobility and affordable tourism!

Seen globally, the market economy principles of capitalism and neoliberalism are intermeshing with each other and mingling with those of current-day Chinese and Russian authoritarian state socialism: growth equals prosperity, for the individual and for as many people as possible. This alliance acts like a catalyst on global warming and climate change[6]: increasing economic growth means more energy demands, more carbon dioxide emissions, more…, more… and more again. But what if the boiler is in danger of blowing up? Addressing economic drivers, and thus climate drivers, in Davos, activist Greta Thunberg spoke urgent words of warning: "Our house is on fire" and "I want you to panic."[7]

Deploying speculative design methods, *After Abundance* responds to the question "What if?" by drafting a possible scenario for Austria around 2050—to be more precise, for an Alpine region that, although based on a fictitious forecast, might look something like this: the 2015 Paris Climate Agreement has failed or been fulfilled only partially, drastic political and social action has been taken and the local population have taken things into their own hands, or resorted to crime, in order to survive: A life after abundance. The contemporary witnesses are people from the village community who tell their everyday stories: how to make rain, how to hack seeds, how to preserve a glacier, how a communal energy network works or how customs can help the needy. *After Abundance* is no dystopian apocalypse. It presents an intrepid population facing up to the challenges of boundless climate change by means of self-empowerment and adaptation, harking back to their regional, cultural roots, developing new abilities and manual skills and taking control over access to knowledge and technology. Instead of panicking or succumbing to fear, the protagonists operate with creativity and a gift for improvisation.

The students and the team headed by Anab Jain at the University of Applied Arts in Vienna were invited to develop an entry based on their *Design Investigations* approach that would take advantage of the Biennale as a laboratory to probe their methods and strategies and to engage in the critical discourse on an international platform. The culturally diverse team represented an Austria of different ethnicities and origins, without requiring an Austrian

Wilder Freiger with Grünauferner (top) and Zuckerhütl with Sulzenauferner (bottom) in the Stubaital in Tyrol photographed by the Alpinist and photographer Werner Heiss around 1970. According to the *2016/17 Glacier Report* of the Austrian Alpine Club, the speed of glacial melt has increased drastically since then.

passport, for example Professor Anab Jain herself. The designer and co-founder of the London-based *Superflux* studio who hails from India, lives in London and teaches in Vienna is regarded as being in the vanguard of the critical and investigative discourse in contemporary design. She represents a current in design that deploys investigative design methods to forecast future developments or generate alternative worlds in search of answers to such pressing questions as the changes brought about by technology and globalisation in the Anthropocene: what future awaits us, what future is possible or plausible, and which would be preferable?[8] A highly influential figure, she will pass on her methodology and knowledge as inspiration to a generation of students at the University of Applied Arts. It seemed obvious to develop this challenging Biennale project concerned with emotion and climate change with a very young generation of designers, as their empathy and expectations regarding a future worth living in are of an existential nature. They are the future!

In addition to the urban studio setting in Vienna, the Werkraum Bregenzerwald in Vorarlberg in the west of Austria served as a base for rural Alpine field research. The traditional knowledge acquired while visiting some of the ninety or so workshops in the collective was of great assistance in exploring questions regarding "tools" and "workshops" fit for the future in a world of limited resources. Excursions to local forests and locations of natural events such as the landslide in Sibratsgfäll in 1999 illustrated the indirect and direct effects of climate change on an Alpine region.[9]

The Biennale project *After Abundance* was not only an emotional journey for everyone involved in terms of the way they deal with climate change. As a tangible installation at Somerset House, it also gave rise to a moment of *emotional disruption* among visitors, triggering their own utopian and dystopian conceptions and associated emotions regarding climate change. For this purpose, the designers assumed the role of writers, investigators, scientists, stage designers, film-makers and more, but not the role of the therapist or healer, nor that of a politician or activist. In order to "save what we can save" of Planet Earth, the global community and all professions will have to get involved. Maybe school-striker Greta Thunberg would see such an extensive learning process as too time-consuming for students in view of the urgent action required to reverse global warming and emissions. In the context of a design biennale, it was above all an experiment intended to probe the possibilities and limits of design and its capacity for inter-disciplinarity—a worthwhile and acclaimed approach.[10]

1—Climate activist Greta Thunberg in Davos "I want you to feel the fear I do. Every day" in: *Spiegel online,* 25 January 2019, last accessed on 27 February 2019.
2—Cf. The United Nations' *Emission Gap Report 2018* or the *Special Report on Global Warming of 1.5 °C* published by the Intergovernmental Panel on Climate Change, IPPC. The two climate researchers Helga Kromp-Kolb and Kate Marvel provide further evidence in this book.
3—Cf. *London Design Biennale 2018 Prospectus,* p. 15.
4—Ibid.
5—In fact 18.1 % of the Austrian population (1,563,000 people) are at risk of poverty or exclusion. Cf. http://www.armutskonferenz.at/armut-in-oesterreich/aktuelle-armuts-und-verteilungszahlen.html, last accessed on 27 February 2019
6—With regard to the links between economic growth and climate change, cf. Nordhaus, William D. (2015) *The Climate Casino: Risk, Uncertainty and Economics for a Warming World.* Yale University Press.
7—Climate activist Greta Thunberg in Davos "I want you to feel the fear I do. Every day" in *Spiegel online,* 25 January 2019, last accessed on 27 February 2019.
8—An account of this approach to design is given, inter alia, in: Dunne, Anthony / Raby, Fiona (2013) *Speculative Everything – Design, Fiction, and Social Dreaming.* MIT Press.
9—An extended period of rainfall in May 1999 caused an entire slope in the municipality of Sibratsgfäll to slide over an area of 1.4 square kilometres, taking an Alpine village with it. Seventeen buildings were destroyed or severely damaged, sixty-five hectares of forest devastated, and eighty-five hectares of Alpine pasture were rendered useless for grazing. Today, the Georunde Rindberg and "Felber's Schiefes Haus" commemorate the disaster. See http://www.bewegtenatur.at/, last accessed on 27 February 2019.
10—The attention attracted by the Austrian entry was also reflected in the international press, cf. "Mind and Body take Centerstage" in: *New York Times,* 4/9/2018; "10 of the best installations at London Design Biennale 2018" in: *Canada Live News,* 4/9/2018.

EMOTIONALE DIS-RUPTION

Thomas   Geisler

„*Was ich auf dieser Konferenz zu erreichen hoffe, ist die Erkenntnis, dass wir einer existenziellen Bedrohung ausgesetzt sind. Dies ist die größte Krise, in der sich die Menschheit je befunden hat. Zuerst müssen wir dies erkennen und dann so schnell wie möglich etwas tun, um die Emissionen aufzuhalten, und versuchen, das zu retten, was wir noch können.*"
Greta Thunberg

Dieser emotionale Weckruf der jungen Schwedin Greta Thunberg erreichte nicht nur die Teilnehmer*innen der UN-Klimakonferenz in Katowice im Dezember 2018, sondern fand seine virale Verbreitung auf der ganzen Welt. Mit einem Schulstreik zur Einhaltung der Klimaziele in ihrem Heimatland löste sie bereits die weltweite Bewegung *Fridays for Future* unter Jugendlichen und Gleichgesinnten aus. Ihren Appell für drastische Veränderungen in der Klimapolitik wiederholte der Teenager gegenüber hochrangigen Politiker*innen und Wirtschaftsexpert*innen anlässlich des Weltwirtschaftsforums 2019 in Davos: „Alle sollen die Angst spüren, die ich selbst jeden Tag spüre!"[1]

Angesichts der im Vorfeld und zur Konferenz in Katowice präsentierten Zahlen und Prognosen für den Fortbestand der Erde und die Auswirkungen durch den Klimawandel müsste es in der Tat jedem vernünftigen Menschen angst und bange werden.[2]

Angst ist wie Freude, Furcht, Liebe oder Hass ein Grundgefühl und laut Evolutionspsychologie in allen Kulturen gleichermaßen anzutreffen. Primäraffekte ermöglichen somit eine auf Emotionen basierende, weltweit verständliche und nonverbale Kommunikation. Eigentlich erstaunlich, dass Thunberg, der das Asperger-Syndrom diagnostiziert wurde, sich in ihren Botschaften der Sprache der Emotionen bedient, wo autistisch veranlagten Personen gerade ein Defizit in der Wahrnehmung und Äußerung emotional bedingter Signale wie Gestik oder Mimik zugeschrieben wird. Reagieren *wir* vielleicht wie Autist*innen in Bezug auf den Klimawandel? Was berührt uns, wenn uns das Aufheizen unseres Planeten kalt lässt?

Emotional States (dt. Gemütslage) lautete das Motto der zweiten London Design Biennale, die vom 4. bis 23. September 2018 stattfand. Im Somerset House am Themseufer präsentierten sich rund 40 Nationen, Regionen und Metropolen aus sechs Kontinenten. In raumgreifenden Installationen und Ausstellungen wurden die aktuellen Strömungen und Befindlichkeiten in Design und seinen angrenzenden künstlerisch-kreativen und forschenden Disziplinen untersucht und verhandelt. Ziel dieser Gesamtschau war es, die Rolle von Design für eine gemeinsame Zukunft

zu erkunden. Zur Erläuterung des Mottos meinte der britische Kurator und künstlerische Leiter der Biennale Christopher Turner: „Emotionen sind universell; die Bedeutungen, die ihnen zugeschrieben werden, sind überall gleich und kennen keine Grenzen. Gut durchdachte gestalterische und technische Lösungen können positive emotionale Erfahrungen und damit Raum für neue soziale Möglichkeiten schaffen, indem sie Verbundenheit und Austausch ermöglichen und sinnstiftende Beziehungen zwischen den Menschen knüpfen."[3]

Auf die Designdisziplin selbstkritisch reflektierend, verwiesen die Veranstalter in ihrer Ausschreibung auf den historischen und gegenwärtigen Umstand, dass mit jedem Problem, das Entwerfer*innen scheinbar lösen, weitere geschaffen werden. Weshalb Designlösungen nicht unbedingt im Technischen oder Materiellen zu suchen seien, sondern im Immateriellen oder im Bereich der Transzendenz lägen. Daraus abgeleitet könnten sich folgende mögliche Fragestellungen für die Erarbeitung von Beiträgen ergeben: Wie kann Design Emotionen hervorrufen, visualisieren, kommunizieren oder gar manipulieren? Wie können Gestalter*innen dazu beitragen, das Engagement bei Bürger*innen und in Gemeinschaften zu unterstützen, indem das Gemeinwohl positiv und emotional gestärkt wird? Im Umkehrschluss lässt sich aber auch fragen, wie Design negative Gefühlszustände wie Angst oder Stress provozieren und adressieren kann? Oder was es bedeutet, wenn Roboter als emotionale Maschinen entwickelt werden? Wäre es möglich, Konsumverhalten und Müllvermeidung emotional in die Richtung der Nachhaltigkeit zu steuern?[4]

Der österreichische Beitrag *After Abundance* (dt. Nach dem Überfluss) zur London Design Biennale 2018 fokussierte auf die Bedeutung von Design vor dem Hintergrund immer knapper werdender Rohstoffe, des Raubbaus an der Natur, extremer Klima- und Wettersituationen und anderer prekärer Entwicklungen durch den Klimawandel, wie sie global und auch in Österreich zu beobachten sind. Die damit weit verbreitete Gemütslage – sowohl bei den Projektbeteiligten wie auch in der Öffentlichkeit – zwischen Angst, Panik, Ratlosigkeit oder Ohnmacht sollte zu einem produktiven, selbstsicheren und ermutigenden Bewusstsein führen. Ein optimistischer Ansatz, der jenen, die diesen komplexen Themen und Herausforderungen mit Gleichgültigkeit oder Verdrängung begegnen, emanzipiert, konstruktiv und aufrüttelnd gegenübertritt.

Gerade in Österreich wähnen wir uns auf einer Insel der Seligen. Nicht nur die wirtschaftlich privilegierte Situation als eines der reichsten EU-Länder, auch die zentralkontinentale Lage im Alpenraum verblendet und verhindert einen Blick auf das, was jenseits des Wohlstands liegt.[5] Der durch den Klimawandel bedingte Anstieg des Meeresspiegels und Tropenstürme machen nicht direkt betroffen, und Dürren scheinen unvorstellbar, da der Wasserreichtum sprudelnder Bergquellen

beruhigend wirkt – wobei auf diesem vergleichsweise kleinen Territorium zwischen Stadt-, Land- und Bergbevölkerung bereits eklatant unterschiedliche Wahrnehmungen festzustellen sind. Denken wir nur an einen der heißen Sommertage in Wien – auch Hundstage genannt – oder im Salzkammergut, wohin viele Städter*innen zur „Sommerfrische" flüchten. Klimawandel-Skeptiker*innen sehen wohl gerade darin eine seit Jahrhunderten gepflegte Tradition oder erkennen eine gesellschaftliche Verbesserung, dass das einst dem Adel und reichen Bürgertum vorbehaltene Privileg, jetzt demokratisiert für (fast) alle möglich ist: der allgemeinen Mobilität und dem Tourismus in allen Preisklassen sei Dank!

Global gesehen greifen die marktwirtschaftlichen Prinzipien von Kapitalismus und Neoliberalismus ineinander und vermischen sich mit jenen des autoritären Staatssozialismus aktueller chinesischer und russischer Prägung: Wachstum ist gleich Wohlstand, für den Einzelnen und für möglichst alle. Die Allianz wirkt dabei wie ein Katalysator auf die Erderwärmung und den Klimawandel: steigendes Wirtschaftswachstum, bedeutet mehr Energiebedarf, mehr CO_2-Ausstoß, mehr …, mehr … und nochmal mehr.[6] Was aber, wenn der Heizkessel zu explodieren droht? Die Aktivistin Greta Thunberg mahnte in Davos gegenüber den Wirtschafts- und somit Klimatreiber*innen in drastischen Worten: „Unser Haus brennt" und „Ich will, dass ihr in Panik geratet."[7]

Mit spekulativen Designmethoden zeichnet *After Abundance* als Antwort auf die Frage „Was wäre wenn?" ein mögliches Szenario von einem Österreich um das Jahr 2050 – konkret von einer Alpenregion, die sich, fiktiv in die Zukunft prognostiziert, so darstellen könnte:

Das Weltklimaabkommen von 2015 in Paris ist gescheitert oder nur teilweise erfüllt, drastische politische und gesellschaftliche Maßnahmen wurden ergriffen und die lokale Bevölkerung agiert autonom oder im Illegalen, um sich am Leben zu erhalten: ein Leben nach dem Überfluss. Die Zeitzeug*innen sind Menschen aus der Dorfgemeinschaft, die ihre alltäglichen Geschichten erzählen: wie sich Regen erzeugen lässt, wie Saatgut manipuliert wird, wie ein Gletscher erhalten wird, wie ein kommunales Energienetzwerk funktioniert oder wie durch Brauchtum den Notleidenden geholfen wird. Dennoch ist *After Abundance* keine dystopische Apokalypse. Es zeigt eine unerschrockene Bevölkerung, die sich durch Selbstermächtigung und Anpassung den Herausforderungen des grenzenlosen Klimawandels stellt, sich dabei ihrer regional-kulturellen Wurzeln besinnt, neue Fähigkeiten und Handfertigkeiten entwickelt und sich dem Zugang zu Wissen und Technologie bemächtigt. Statt in Panik oder Angst agieren die Akteur*innen mit Kreativität und Improvisationsgabe.

Die Studierenden und das Team rund um Anab Jain von der Universität für angewandte Kunst in Wien waren eingeladen, mit ihrem Gestaltungsansatz der *Design Investigations,* einen Beitrag zu entwickeln, der die Biennale als Labor zum Ausloten ihrer Methoden und Ansätze nutzt und sich dem kritischen Diskurs einer internationalen Plattform stellt. Das kulturell diverse Team vertrat dabei ein Österreich verschiedener Ethnien und Herkünfte ohne notwendigen Nachweis eines österreichischen Passes wie im Fall der Professorin Anab Jain selbst. Die aus Indien stammende, in London lebende und in Wien unterrichtende Designerin und Mitbegründerin des Londoner Studios *Superflux* gilt als eine der renommiertesten Vertreter*innen in der kritischen und investigativen Auseinandersetzung im zeitgenössischen Design. Dabei vertritt sie eine Strömung im Design, die durch investigative Gestaltungsmethoden Zukunftsprognosen abgibt oder alternative Welten imaginiert. So versucht sie, Antworten auf dringliche Fragen wie die Veränderungen durch Technologie und Globalisierung im Anthropozän zu finden: Welche Zukunft erwartet uns, welche ist möglich oder plausibel und was wäre zu bevorzugen?[8] Als prägende Persönlichkeit wird sie einer Generation von Studierenden an der Angewandten ihre Arbeitsweise und Wissen als Inspiration weitergeben. Das herausfordernde Biennale-Projekt zu Emotion und Klimawandel mit einer sehr jungen Generation von Designer*innen zu erarbeiten, lag dabei auf der Hand, da deren Empathie und Erwartungen an eine lebenswerte Zukunft existenzieller Natur sind. Sie sind die Zukunft!

Neben dem urbanen Studioumfeld Wiens diente der Werkraum Bregenzerwald in Vorarlberg im westlichen Österreich der ländlich-alpinen Feldforschung. In der Auseinandersetzung mit den Fragestellungen zu zukunftsfähigen „Werkzeugen" und „Werkstätten" für eine Welt begrenzter Ressourcen, half das tradierte Wissen beim Besuch von einer Handvoll der rund 90 Handwerksbetriebe des Kollektivs. Exkursionen in die Wälder der Region und an Schauplätze von Naturereignissen, wie dem Hangrutsch in Sibratsgfäll von 1999, vermittelten die mittelbaren und unmittelbaren Auswirkungen des Klimawandels auf eine Alpenregion.[9]

Das Biennale-Projekt *After Abundance* war nicht nur eine emotionale Reise für jede*n Mitwirkende*n im eigenen Umgang mit dem Klimawandel, sondern erfüllte als sinnlich erfahrbare Installation im Somerset House bei den Besucher*innen ein Moment Emotionaler Disruption: Ausgelöst wurden eigene utopische und dystopische Vorstellungen und die damit verbundenen Empfindungen zum Klimawandel. Dafür schlüpften die beteiligten Designer*innen in die Rolle von Schriftsteller*innen, Ermittler*innen, Wissenschaftler*innen, Bühnenbildner*innen, Filmemacher*innen und viele mehr – nicht jedoch, in die von Therapeut*innen oder Heiler*innen, auch nicht in die von Politiker*innen und Aktivist*innen. Um vom Planeten Erde „das zu retten, was wir noch können", bedarf es der Mitwirkung der Globalgemeinschaft und aller Professionen. Mag sein, dass Greta Thunberg als Schulverweigerin einen solch umfangreichen Lernprozess für Studierende als zu zeitaufwändig in Bezug auf die dringlichen Maßnahmen zur Abkehr der Erderwärmung und Emissionen sehen würde. Im Kontext einer Design Biennale war es vor allem ein Experiment, die Möglichkeiten und Grenzen von Design und seiner Fähigkeit zur Interdisziplinarität auszuloten – ein lohnender und viel beachteter Weg.[10]

1—Klimaaktivistin Greta Thunberg in Davos „Alle sollen die Angst spüren, die ich selbst jeden Tag spüre". In: *Spiegel online*, 25.01.2019 [aufgerufen am 27.02.2019].
2—Vgl. *Emission Gap Report 2018* der Vereinten Nationen, oder der *Sonderbericht 1,5 °C globale Erwärmung* des Weltklimarats IPPC. Die beiden Klimaforscherinnen Helga Kromp-Kolb und Kate Marvel in diesem Buch geben weitere Zeugnisse.
3—Vgl. *Prospectus London Design Biennale 2018*, S. 15.
4—Ebenda.
5—Laut Armutskonferenz sind 18,1 % der österreichischen Bevölkerung (1.563.000 Menschen) armuts- oder ausgrenzungsgefährdet. Vgl. http://www.armutskonferenz.at/armut-in-oesterreich/aktuelle-armuts-und-verteilungszahlen.html [aufgerufen am 27.02.2019].
6—Für die Zusammenhänge von Wirtschaftswachstum und Klimawandel vgl. Nordhaus, William D. (2015) *The Climate Casino: Risk, Uncertainty and Economics for a Warming World.* Yale University Press.
7—Wie 1.
8—Eine Entwicklungsgeschichte dieses Designansatzes findet sich u.a. in Dunne, Anthony / Raby, Fiona (2013) *Speculative Everything – Design, Fiction, and Social Dreaming.* MIT Press.
9—Nach einer langen Regenperiode im Mai 1999 geriet auf einem Areal von 1,4 km² auf dem Gemeindegebiet von Sibratsgfäll ein ganzer Hang samt Almdorf in Bewegung. 17 Gebäude wurden zerstört oder schwer beschädigt, 65 Hektar Wald vernichtet, 85 Hektar Almfläche als Weideland unbrauchbar. Heute erinnert die Georunde Rindberg und Felber's Schiefes Haus an die Katastrophe. Vgl. http://www.bewegtenatur.at/ [aufgerufen am 27.02.2019].
10—Die Aufmerksamkeit für den Österreich-Beitrag schlug sich auch in der internationalen Presse nieder, vgl. Mind and Body take Centerstage. In: *New York Times*, 04.09.2018; 10 of the best installations at London Design Biennale 2018. In: *Canada Live News*, 04.09.2018.

WHY DESIGN INVESTI-GATIONS?

Anab Jain

I grew up in a family of educators. I saw the relentless energy and humility that came with teaching, from the interactions between my parents and their students. Despite this early insight into the rewards of pedagogy as a profession, I somehow convinced myself that my doggedness and impatience were not fit for teaching. Many years later, as a student of design at the Royal College of Art in London, I encountered the prolific blog of architect and educator Lebbeus Woods. Woods wrote voraciously about his role as an educator in challenging *normality* at times of complexity and uncertainty. His writing had a deep influence during my formative years as a student and later as a design practitioner.

Now, almost two decades later, I realise it is the passion of my parents, and the sagacious writings of Woods that have shaped my teaching philosophy at *Design Investigations*. The constant question that underpins my pedagogical approach is: When everything is shifting: technological constructs, political situations, financial structures, ecological systems, what is the evolving role of a designer? As far as possible, our program seeks to prepare students for investigating the opportunities and unintended consequences of such accelerated change. I believe our job at DI is to expand our students' capacity to produce tools, tactics and narratives that catalyse critical thinking and transformative action towards a more hopeful and humane future. My teaching colleagues and I continually foster an open-ended, critically, politically and socially relevant creative environment for our students as far as we can within the legislative and economic boundaries of the University. We hope to spark their imaginations, nurture their ambitions and become a guiding vision in the directions they wish to pursue. Because as Woods[1] articulated so clearly, "A true education, would be one which keeps itself aware of the shifts and changes of the world, whilst allowing the freedom for thinking and learning outside of mere supply and demand, investment and product."

A recurring theme that every design practitioner must face in years to come will be climate change, and our relationship to the natural world. I strongly believe that confronting our fears and anxieties, and experimenting with ways we can address the shocks and disruptions of climate change has become an essential requirement and skill for designers. The *After Abundance* brief is a response to that requirement. For this brief we asked students to explore and investigate a post-abundant Austria—an Austria that has transitioned from abundance to scarcity as a consequence of climate change. This context, territory, and landscape was familiar to many of our students, it was their current Heimat. This is a chronicle of the projects our students did in response to the brief, which was presented as Austria's official entry to the London Design Biennale 2018.

We launched the brief with an anthropological field trip to the Alpine regions of Bregenzerwald in the state of Vorarlberg. In Sibratsgfäll we visited the home of a community leader, whose house tilted precariously on the side of a mountain, physically shifted by unprecedented landslides. This vertigo-inducing home had become a reminder of the community's enduring resilience in the face of extreme natural events. Guided into the nearby woods by a forester we discovered fir trees succumbing to rising temperatures, revealing the fragility of the Alpine forest. We visited quarries, community centres and craft making spaces. Beneath the seeming calm and wealth, festered an unsettling sense of uncertainty about the region's future in the face of climate change. Yet we heard stories of enduring resilience and interdependence and it became apparent that the future would be neither a linear extrapolation of utopia or dystopia. Our task

was to decipher the interconnected nature of ecological, political, economic and social systems and design signposts that help navigate through these complex presents and futures.

In the subsequent months of experimentation, our students developed concepts, tested prototypes, built scale models, investigated materials, wrote stories; finding their way through the tangle of troubles and creativity of the Anthropocene. What emerged from this process exceeded all my expectations. Our installation, *After Abundance* at the London Design Biennale 2018 was neither a technological fix or a

design solution but a poignant, granular and multilayered concurrence of hacks, questions and entangled narratives of hope and unease, renewal and destruction, law and penalty, justice and refusal, rage and joy—the multitudes that might define life in the Alpine region in the face of imminent climate extremities.

Upon entering the *After Abundance* installation visitors are transported into an Alpine landscape, encountering a world contending with the stark realities of climate change. From a drone producing illegal rain to a corn cartel run in a by a retired bio-hacker turned social activist, the immersive scenes give an arresting glimpse of life in a changed rural Austria. Further along, visitors are confronted by larger than life costumes of beasts and monsters made from straw, wood, abandoned plastic, and waste materials. Once the cacophony of horns, bells, and yelled instructions subsides, the audience bear witness to the final minutes of an Alpine custom that has been revived as a social protest movement. The Heische costumes are a stark reminder of how our pasts will always haunt our presents. As Anna Tsing[2] says, "It's a haunting with all the things you can't leave behind, in contrast to the modernist dream that you can break from the past,"and I would add, that the future will be an untouched blank slate where everything will be new and shiny. Up ahead, framed by mountains, is the stoic face of a melting glacier sounding out a haunting siren. Figures clad in white pick their way across the ice, spraying water in

a poignant effort to arrest its decline and restore its dignity. Inspired by vernacular traditions of understanding the world, these speculative investigations portray a moving glimpse of how an Alpine community might use craft and cunning to thrive in a landscape altered by climate change.

As designers who will become practitioners in years to come, the students who produced the exhibition *After Abundance* show us what it means to acknowledge the limits of anthropocentric capitalism and embrace the burden of a world that is increasingly complex and challenging. And, more importantly what commitment is required to propose alternate forms of design, critical activism, social justice and multispecies solidarity.

Being an educator is my way of signing up to lifelong learning. My students are my teachers, and their discerning optimism is my hope for the future.

1—Woods, L. (2011) Why Cooper Union Matters. Available at: https://lebbeuswoods.wordpress.com/2011/12/12/why-cooper-union-matters/
2—Tsing, A. (2017) The Best of End Times: A Conversation with Anna Tsing by Charles Carlin. Available at: http://edgeeffects.net/anna-tsing/

In 1999, the idyllic mountain village of Sibratsgfäll in Bregenzerwald was affected by a gigantic landslide: on an area of around 1.6 square kilometres, the mountainsides on the Rindberg plot started moving inexorably, with 18 buildings sliding down to the valley, some houses moving from their original spot by up to 240 metres. We visited Georunde Rindberg, a lone titling cube that stands as a memorial of the landslide, and ongoing geological shifts. We learnt how people in Sibratsgfäll have invented new ways of living with the forces of nature, building houses which can move, which can slide along with the earth. The nature trail was awarded the 2017 Austrian State Prize for Design in the category Spatial Design.

W A R U M

DESIGN
INVESTIGATIONS

Anab Jain   ?

Ich komme aus einer Familie von Pädagog*innen. In der Interaktion zwischen meinen Eltern und ihren Studierenden erlebte ich die unermüdliche Energie und Demut, die mit dem Unterrichten verbunden sind. Obwohl ich also früh erkannte, welch lohnende Tätigkeit die Pädagogik darstellt, musste ich mir eingestehen, dass meine Zielstrebigkeit und Ungeduld einem Lehrberuf im Wege stünden. Jahre später stieß ich als Designstudentin am Londoner Royal College of Art auf den ausführlichen Blog des Architekten und Lehrers Lebbeus Woods, der unermüdlich von seiner Rolle berichtete, als Lehrender in unsicheren und komplexen Zeiten die *Normalität* in Frage zu stellen. Seine Texte beeinflussten nicht nur meine Entwicklung als Studentin nachhaltig, sondern auch meine spätere Arbeit als Designerin.

Heute – nahezu zwei Jahrzehnte später – erkenne ich, wie sehr die Leidenschaft meiner Eltern und Woods' scharfsinnige Gedanken meine Unterrichtsphilosophie im Rahmen der *Design Investigations* prägen. Die beharrliche Frage, die meinem pädagogischen Ansatz zugrunde liegt, lautet: Wie entwickelt sich die Rolle von Designer*innen, wenn alles – technologische Konstrukte, politische Situationen, Finanzstrukturen, ökologische Systeme – in Veränderung begriffen ist?

Unser Programm bereitet die Studierenden so gut wie möglich darauf vor, sich mit den Chancen und unbeabsichtigten Folgen dieses forcierten Veränderungsprozesses auseinanderzusetzen. Ich denke, es ist unsere Aufgabe, die Studierenden zur Schaffung von Instrumenten, von Taktiken und Narrativen zu befähigen, die kritisches Denken und transformatives Handeln mit Blick auf eine hoffnungsvollere, humanere Zukunft ermöglichen. Meine Kolleg*innen und ich bemühen uns, im Rahmen der rechtlichen und budgetären Möglichkeiten der Universität eine offene, kritische und kreative Studienumgebung zu fördern, die politisch und gesellschaftlich relevant ist. Wir möchten die Fantasie unserer Studierenden beflügeln, sie in ihren Zielen unterstützen und Leitbilder für die von ihnen angestrebte Entwicklung sein. Wie Lebbeus Woods so klarsichtig erkannte: „Jede echte Ausbildung ist sich der Veränderungen und Umbrüche der Welt bewusst und schafft gleichzeitig einen Freiraum, der es ermöglicht, über Angebot und Nachfrage, Investition und Produkt hinaus zu denken und zu lernen."[1]

Der Klimawandel und unser Verhältnis zur natürlichen Umwelt sind Themen, mit denen Designer*innen in Zukunft immer wieder konfrontiert sein werden. Ich bin überzeugt davon, dass die Auseinandersetzung mit Ängsten und Befürchtungen und das Experimentieren mit Bewältigungsstrategien für die durch den Klimawandel verursachten Disruptionen und Erschütterungen grundlegende Anforderungen und Fähigkeiten moderner Designer*innen darstellen. Mit *After Abundance* stellt sich *Design Investigations* dieser Notwendigkeit. Die Studierenden wurden aufgefordert zu erkunden, wie Österreich nach dem Überfluss aussehen könnte – ein Österreich, das aufgrund des Klimawandels nicht länger von Fülle, sondern von Mangel gekennzeichnet ist. Kontext, Territorium und Landschaft sind vielen unserer Studierenden als ihre aktuelle Heimat vertraut. In dieser Publikation sollen die Projekte vorgestellt werden, die die Studierenden als Antwort auf die Einladung entworfen haben, Österreichs offiziellen Beitrag zur London Design Biennale 2018 beizusteuern.

Ausgangspunkt des Designprozesses war eine anthropologische Exkursion in die alpine Region des Bregenzerwaldes in Vorarlberg. In Sibratsgfäll besuchten wir das Haus eines führenden Gemeindemitglieds, das im Zuge eines beispiellosen Erdrutsches den Berghang hinunterglitt und sich heute in gefährlicher Schräglage befindet. Dieses im Inneren Schwindel erregende Gebäude wurde zum Mahnmal für die beharrliche Widerstandskraft der lokalen Gemeinschaft angesichts extremer Naturereignisse. Geführt von einem Förster entdeckten wir im nahegelegenen Wald die Auswirkungen der steigenden Temperaturen auf die Tannen, was uns die Verletzlichkeit des alpinen Waldes vor Augen führte. Wir besuchten Steinbrüche, Gemeindezentren und Werkstätten. Trotz scheinbarer Ruhe und Wohlstands war ein verstörendes Gefühl der Unsicherheit in Bezug auf die Zukunft der Region in Zeiten des Klimawandels zu spüren. Doch wir hörten auch Geschichten, die von Widerstandskraft und wechselseitiger Unterstützung erzählten, und es wurde klar, dass sich die Zukunft nicht linear als Utopie oder Dystopie ableiten lässt. Unsere Aufgabe bestand darin, die Vernetzungen ökologischer, politischer, ökonomischer und sozialer Systeme zu entschlüsseln und Wegweiser für die Reise durch diese vielschichtige Gegenwart und Zukunft zu entwerfen.

Es folgten Monate des Experimentierens, in denen unsere Studierenden Konzepte entwickelten, Prototypen testeten, maßstabsgetreue Modelle bauten, Materialien erforschten und Geschichten verfassten; dabei lernten sie, ihren Weg durch das Wirrwarr an Problemen und kreativen Potenzialen des Anthropozäns zu finden. Das Ergebnis überstieg alle meine Erwartungen. Die bei der London Design Biennale 2018 präsentierte Installation *After Abundance* war weder eine technologische Anpassung noch eine Designlösung. In überwältigender, detaillierter und vielschichtiger Form verknüpfte sie Problemlösungen und Fragen mit komplexen Erzählungen über Hoffnung und Unbehagen, Erneuerung und Zerstörung, Recht und Strafe, Gerechtigkeit und Verweigerung, Zorn und Freude – die ganze Vielfalt an Aspekten also, die das Leben in den Alpen angesichts drohender Klimaextreme bestimmen könnten.

Mit dem Betreten der Installation *After Abundance* werden die Besucher*innen in eine alpine Landschaft versetzt, in eine Welt, die mit der düsteren Realität des Klimawandels kämpft. Von einer Drohne, die verbotenen Regen erzeugt, bis zum Maiskartell, das von einer ehemaligen Biohackerin und nunmehrigen Sozialaktivistin in einem Schuppen betrieben wird – die eindringlichen Szenarien gewähren spannende Einblicke in das Leben eines veränderten ländlichen Österreichs. Ein Stück weiter treffen die Besucher*innen auf überlebensgroße Kostüme von wilden Tieren und Monstern aus Stroh, Holz, weggeworfenem Plastik und Abfallstoffen. Wenn die Kakophonie aus Hörnern, Schellen und gebrüllten Anweisungen verklingt, erlebt das Publikum die letzten Minuten eines alpinen Brauchtums, das als soziale Protestbewegung zu neuem Leben erweckt wurde. Die Heische-Kostüme führen uns schonungslos vor Augen, dass die Gegenwart unweigerlich von der Vergangenheit heimgesucht wird. Um es mit Anna Tsing zu sagen: „Es ist eine Heimsuchung mit all den Dingen, die wir nicht zurücklassen können, im Gegensatz zum modernistischen Traum, sich von der Vergangenheit loslösen zu können."[2] Ich möchte dem hinzufügen, dass die Zukunft ein unberührtes und unbeschriebenes Blatt sein wird, auf dem alles in neuem Glanz erstrahlt. Vor uns sehen wir, umrahmt von Bergen, das gleichmütige Antlitz eines schmelzenden Gletschers, begleitet vom eindringlichen Ton einer Sirene. Im ergreifenden Bemühen, den Rückgang des Gletschers zu stoppen und ihm seine Würde zurückzugeben, suchen weiß gekleidete Figuren vorsichtig einen Weg über das Eis und versprühen Wasser. Diese spekulativen Erkundungen vermitteln – inspiriert von lokalen Traditionen, die Welt zu sehen – einen berührenden Eindruck davon, wie sich eine alpine Gemeinschaft mit Geschick und Findigkeit in einer vom Klimawandel transformierten Landschaft behaupten könnte.

Als Designer*innen, die diesen Beruf in Zukunft aktiv ausüben werden, zeigen uns die Studierenden hinter der Ausstellung *After Abundance,* was es bedeutet, sich der Grenzen des menschgemachten Kapitalismus anzunehmen und sich der Bürde einer immer komplexeren und herausfordernderen Welt zu stellen. Und – was noch wichtiger ist – sie führen uns vor Augen, welches Engagement es braucht, um alternative Zugänge zu Design und kritischem Aktivismus, sozialer Gerechtigkeit und speziesübergreifender Solidarität zu entwickeln.

Das Unterrichten ist meine Form des lebenslangen Lernens. Meine Studierenden sind meine Lehrer*innen, in ihrem kritischen Optimismus liegt meine Hoffnung für die Zukunft.

1—Woods, L. (2011) Why Cooper Union Matters. Siehe: https://lebbeuswoods. wordpress.com/2011/12/12/why-cooper-union-matters/
2—Tsing, A. (2017) The Best of End Times: A Conversation with Anna Tsing by Charles Carlin. Siehe: http://edgeeffects.net/anna-tsing/

THE SCIENCE OF CLIMATE CHANGE
Helga Kromp-Kolb

Taking abundance to indicate "the world as we know it", we find that science is not the best place to look for information about the future. When Donella and Dennis Meadows and their co-authors published the report "Limits to Growth"[1] in 1972, they were careful to point out that their model could simulate global developments up to the point of collapse, but not beyond; and although the graphs continue, they lack significance. Current climate scenarios typically show systematic changes, such as increasing temperatures or decreasing precipitation, but in general they do not include disruptive events or tipping points, although there is increasing evidence that these will occur.[2] The more general studies on planetary boundaries focus on defining and staying within the boundaries, even flourishing within them, not on what lies beyond.[3] Does this mean that science can tell us nothing about the time after abundance? Surely not.

In the first place, most of the world's population has never experienced abundance, affluence or wealth. Thus a lack of abundance can be observed right now in the real world—no need for prognostic scientific studies. While, however, in the diction of Herman Daly[4], the world was still empty, it was easier to live a fulfilled, an abundant life, even if conditions were harsh and work was hard. In the full world, with so many people crowding a small global ecosystem and demanding more and more resources, things are different. Ingenious and industrious engineers and entrepreneurs have ruined livelihoods through their immediate interference with the ecosystem—such as the diversion of water from the Caspian Sea in order to grow cotton, the introduction of commercially attractive fish to Lake Victoria, or dirty oil drilling in Nigeria. Meanwhile, climate change has had an even greater impact: only about 5% of the original surface of Lake Chad remains, the rest having evaporated. Thus a large part of the eight million people dependent on Lake Chad have lost their means of sustenance, forcing them to migrate, or delivering them to terror organisations such as Boko Haram. The now unreliable arrival of the monsoon has had a similarly devastating effect in other parts of Africa and in Asia. Arriving in Europe as victims of climate change, these migrants are labelled "economic refugees" and are not welcomed.

But even where abundance currently exists, it might well come to an end long before ecological boundaries are crossed, before a collapse or a tipping-point is reached. The changes anticipated are clearly described in the succession of IPCC reports[5]: Food and water scarcity leading to hunger and poverty; floods and flash floods along large rivers and small streams; heavy storms and increasingly energetic tropical cyclones in coastal areas. The retreat of glaciers and thawing of permafrost are resulting in the destabilisation of mountain slopes and a loss of infrastructure in colder regions. A rise in sea levels and the inward movement of salt water will force tens of millions to migrate within the next few decades. Even in little Austria—unaffected by rising sea levels or tropical storms , and rarely hit by extensive droughts—the costs are estimated to reach 8 billion euros per year, i.e. roughly 2% of GDP by the middle of the century, if climate change is not curbed.[6]

On the other hand, science, in a general way, can tell us quite a bit about what will happen to the Earth if we do cross the line. One of the most relevant issues is that positive feedback processes will lead to continuous warming, irrespective of what measures are taken. Coming generations will face a systematically warming world to which they can only try to adapt. There will be no way to stop the warming before a new equilibrium is reached at a temperature level that will not sustain 11 billion humans.

But the present and future evils described are not a matter of fate. The industrialised, richer part of the human population could voluntarily choose to end its abundance in resource use, thereby providing at least "enough" for the others and for future generations.[7] A future resulting from system changes as promoted by many NGOs, as well as some more progressive scientists and politicians, would take the aims of the UN 2030 Agenda for Sustainable Development and its 17 Sustainable Development Goals seriously, connecting the two essential agendas, the human security agenda and the planetary boundaries agenda synergistically and avoiding competition between them—while at the same time leaving no one behind. What system changes would be required? Some of the changes for industrialised nations are trivial: If active mobility, i.e. walking, cycling and public transport are incentivised, then people's health improves, the number of accidents falls, parents need not drive their children to school, music lessons and sports activities. Mobility becomes more communicative, air quality and noise improve, there is more space for trees in cities, parks and playgrounds, greenhouse gas emissions are reduced and savings are made in infrastructure, the health system and energy.[8] Similarly small shifts in diet towards more generic, local vegetables, to seasonal fruit and grains can entail multiple benefits: Less fat and protein is healthier; no pesticides, antibiotics or unwanted hormones are taken up through food; products ripened in the sun taste better; fewer animals suffer; soils can recover and store more carbon, more water and sustain more biodiversity—resulting in greater resilience to the adverse effects of climate change, while making agricultural yields more reliable for farmers. At the same time, building up humus is a prime measure to combat climate change. Multiple co-benefits can be reaped by changes in clothing and leisure habits, adaptations to buildings and many other domains. A key issue is the replacement of an economic system whose stability depends on growth and whose declared aim is to maximise monetary profits, which

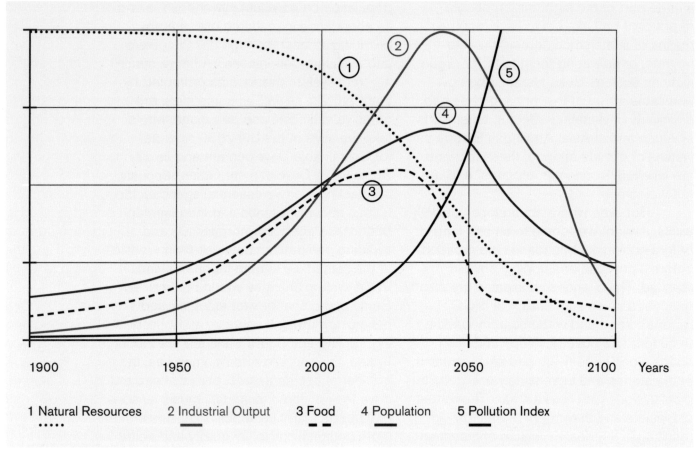

1 Natural Resources   2 Industrial Output   3 Food   4 Population   5 Pollution Index

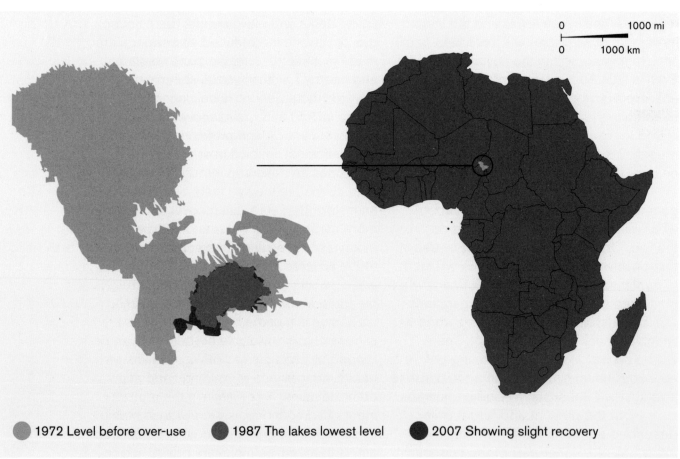

● 1972 Level before over-use   ● 1987 The lakes lowest level   ● 2007 Showing slight recovery

tends to monetise everything and to profit from fragmentation and economies of scale and which assumes that individually optimised solutions are also optimal for society as a whole.[9] Of comparable importance is the restructuring of a financial and monetary system that has by far outgrown the real economy, and which has rules in place for the systematic redistribution of wealth and income from the poorer to the richer.[10]

Summing up, the world as we know it is still rooted in the industrialised world, but many are already experiencing the disastrous future that lies ahead of us unless we reconsider and rapidly readjust our trajectory. Scientists should leave their ivory tower and join in the common effort for a future with a vastly different, and much more meaningful, abundance.

1—Meadows, Dennis / Meadows, Donella / Zahn, Erich / Milling, Peter (1972) *The Limits to Growth. A report to the Club of Rome,* A Potomac Associates Book.
Raworth, K. (2018) *Doughnut Economics: Seven Ways to Think Like a 21st-Century Economist,* Random House Business.
2—Spratt, D. / Dunlop, I. (2018) What lies Beneath. The Understatement Of Existential Climate Risk. Breakthrough.
3—Rockström, J. / Steffen, W. et al. (2009) A safe operating space for humanity. In: *Nature,* 461, 472.
Steffen, W. / Richardson, Katherine / Rockström, Johan et al. (2015) Planetary boundaries: Guiding human development on a changing planet. In: *Science* 349, 1286-1287.
Steffen, W. / Rockström, J. et al. (2018) Trajectories of the Earth System in the Anthropocene. *Proceedings of the National Academy of Sciences.*
4—Daly, H. (1992) Vom Wirtschaften in einer leeren Welt zum Wirtschaften in einer vollen Welt. In: Goodland / Daly / Serafy / Droste (Hg.) *Nach dem Brundtland-Bericht: Umweltverträgliche Wirtschaftliche Entwicklung.* Bonn: Rheinischer Landwirtschaftsverlag.
Daly, H. (2015) Economics for a Full World. *The Great Transition Initiative.*
5—IPCC (2014) Climate Change 2014: Synthesis Report. Contribution of Working Groups I, II and III to the Fifth Assessment Report of the Intergovernmental Panel on Climate Change [Core Writing Team, R. K. Pachauri and L. A. Meyer (eds.)]. Geneva, Switzerland, IPCC.
6—Steininger, K. / König, Martin / Bednar-Friedl, Birgit / Kranzl, Lukas / Loibl, Wolfgang / Prettenthaler, Franz (2014) *Economic Evaluation of Climate Change Impacts. Development of a Cross-Sectoral Framework and Results for Austria,* Heidelberg New York Dordrecht London: Springer.
7—Weizsäcker, E. U. v. / Wijkman, A. et al. (2018) *Come On! Capitalism, Short-termism, Population and the Destruction of the Planet. A Report to the Club of Rome.* New York: Springer Science.
8—APCC (2018) Pre-Print Österreichischer Special Report Gesundheit, Demographie und Klimawandel, Austrian Special Report 2018 (ASR18). *In:* (APCC), A. P. O. C. C. (ed.). Vienna, Austria.
9—Raworth, K. (2018) *Doughnut Economics: Seven Ways to Think Like a 21st-Century Economist,* Random House Business.
10—Lietaer, Bernard / Arnsperger, Christian / Goerner, Sally / Brunnhuber, Stefan (2013) Money and Sustainability. The Missing Link. THE CLUB OF ROME – EU CHAPTER to Finance Watch and the World Business Academy.

The Limits to Growth. A report to the Club of Rome, 1972.

Lake Chad map showing receding water area and level 1972-2007.

DIE WISSENSCHAFT DES KLIMAWANDELS

Helga Kromp-Kolb

Wenn unter „Überfluss" im Wesentlichen die Welt „wie wir sie kennen" verstanden wird, dann erweist sich die Wissenschaft nicht als beste Quelle für Informationen über unsere Zukunft. Als Donella und Dennis Meadows ihre Studie *Die Grenzen des Wachstums*[1] veröffentlichten, wiesen sie und ihre Koautoren wohlweislich darauf hin, dass ihr Rechenmodell die globalen Entwicklungen bis zum Zeitpunkt des Zusammenbruchs simulieren kann, nicht jedoch die Entwicklung darüber hinaus. Die zugehörigen Kurven brechen zwar nicht unvermittelt ab, doch haben sie jenseits des Kollaps keine Aussagekraft mehr. Moderne Klimaszenarien beschreiben üblicherweise systematische Veränderungen, wie etwa steigende Temperaturen oder verminderte Niederschläge, berücksichtigen jedoch nur selten disruptive Ereignisse oder Kipppunkte, obwohl sich die Anzeichen für deren Auftreten mehren.[2] Allgemeinere Untersuchungen zur Belastbarkeit der Erde konzentrieren sich auf das Erkennen und die Einhaltung ökologischer Grenzen – oder auf eine gedeihliche Entwicklung innerhalb derselben –, nicht auf Entwicklungen jenseits der Grenzen.[3] Kann uns die Wissenschaft also nichts über ein Leben nach dem Überfluss lehren? Ganz so ist es nicht.

Zunächst einmal kennt der Großteil der Weltbevölkerung gar keinen Überfluss, Wohlstand oder Reichtum. Der Mangel an Überfluss ist Teil unserer modernen Welt – da erübrigen sich also wissenschaftliche Prognosen. In einer leeren Welt, um Herman Daly[4] zu zitieren, war es freilich einfacher, ein erfülltes Leben, ein Leben im Überfluss, zu führen, auch wenn die Bedingungen schwierig und die Arbeit hart war. In unserer vollen Welt – in der sich viele Menschen ein kleines globales Ökosystem teilen und immer mehr Ressourcen beanspruchen – stellt sich dies anders dar. Tüchtige und einfallsreiche Ingenieur*innen und Unternehmer*innen haben mittels direkter Eingriffe in das Ökosystem viele Lebensgrundlagen zerstört, etwa durch die Umleitung von Wasser aus dem Kaspischen Meer für den Anbau von Baumwolle, durch die Ansiedlung einer wirtschaftlich einträglichen Fischart im Viktoriasee oder durch umweltschädliche Ölbohrungen in Nigeria. Als noch wirksamer erweist sich mittlerweile der Klimawandel: Der Tschadsee, der einst acht Millionen Menschen ernährte, ist durch Verdunstung auf 5 % seiner ursprünglichen Fläche geschrumpft. In der Folge verlor ein Großteil der Bevölkerung die Lebensgrundlage und war zur Emigration gezwungen oder schloss sich Terrororganisationen

wie Boko Haram an. Ähnlich verheerende Auswirkungen hat die zunehmende Unzuverlässigkeit des Monsuns auf Teile Afrikas sowie Asiens. Opfer des Klimawandels, die sich als Migrant*innen nach Europa aufmachen, werden als „Wirtschaftsflüchtlinge" abgestempelt und sind hier nicht willkommen.

Doch selbst dort, wo heute Überfluss herrscht, könnte dieser lange vor dem Überschreiten der Grenzen und Erreichen der Kipppunkte, lange vor dem Kollaps, zu Ende gehen. Eine umfassende Beschreibung der zu erwartenden Veränderungen findet sich in den fortlaufenden IPCC-Berichten[5]: Hunger und Armut, verursacht durch einen Mangel an Nahrungsmitteln und Wasser; Überschwemmungen und Sturzfluten entlang großer Flüsse und kleinerer Wasserläufe; schwere Stürme und zunehmend heftigere tropische Wirbelstürme in Küstenregionen. Destabilisierung von Berghängen und Infrastrukturverluste in kälteren Regionen durch den Rückzug der Gletscher und das Auftauen von Permafrostböden. Millionen von Menschen, die in den nächsten Jahrzehnten durch den Anstieg des Meeresspiegels und das Vordringen von Salzwasser ins Landesinnere zur Migration gezwungen sein werden. Selbst das kleine Österreich, das von steigenden Meeresspiegeln und tropischen Wirbelstürmen gar nicht und von großflächigen Dürren nur selten betroffen ist, muss bis zur Mitte des Jahrhunderts mit Kosten in Höhe von acht Milliarden Euro jährlich – etwa 2 % des BIP – rechnen, wenn dem Klimawandel nicht Einhalt geboten wird.[6]

Andererseits kann uns die Wissenschaft in allgemeiner Form einiges darüber erzählen, wie sich die Erde entwickeln wird, wenn wir die Rote Linie überschreiten. Besonders bedeutsam ist die Tatsache, dass positive Rückkopplungen die Erwärmung kontinuierlich vorantreiben werden, ungeachtet aller Gegenmaßnahmen. Zukünftige Generationen werden einer systematisch wärmeren Welt gegenüberstehen und können nur versuchen, sich an die neuen Gegebenheiten anzupassen. Es gibt keine Möglichkeit, die Erwärmung zu stoppen, ehe ein neues Gleichgewicht erreicht ist – auf einem Temperaturniveau, das die Ernährung von elf Milliarden Menschen unmöglich macht.

Aber die gegenwärtigen und künftigen Übel sind nicht Schicksal. Die wohlhabende Bevölkerung in den Industriestaaten könnte aus freien Stücken beschließen, ihren übermäßigen Ressourcenverbrauch zu reduzieren und auf diese Weise „genug" für den Rest der Menschheit sowie künftige Generationen sicherzustellen.[7] Eine Zukunft, die auf den von vielen NGOs sowie einigen fortschrittlichen Wissenschaftler*innen und Politiker*innen propagierten Systemveränderungen beruht, nimmt die UN-Agenda 2030 für nachhaltige Entwicklung mit ihren siebzehn „Nachhaltigen Entwicklungszielen" ernst. Sie verknüpft die zwei wesentlichen Anliegen – ein Gutes Leben für alle sicherzustellen und die Belastungsgrenzen unseres Planeten zu respektieren – auf synergistische Weise, ohne sie gegeneinander auszuspielen,

wobei niemand zurückgelassen werden soll. Welche Systemveränderungen wären dazu erforderlich? Manche Maßnahmen in den Industriestaaten erweisen sich als trivial: Anreize zur Förderung aktiver Mobilitätsformen (Gehen, Radfahren, öffentlicher Verkehr) verbessern die Gesundheit der Bevölkerung und vermindern die Unfallhäufigkeit. Eltern müssen ihre Kinder nicht mehr mit dem Auto zur Schule, zum Musikunterricht oder zum Sport bringen; die Kommunikation wird gefördert, die Luftqualität verbessert und der Lärm reduziert. Städte haben mehr Platz für Bäume, Parks und Spielplätze; die Treibhausgasemissionen sinken ebenso wie die Aufwendungen für Infrastruktur, Gesundheitswesen und Energie.[8] Ähnlich geringfügige Veränderungen unseres Speiseplans – mehr Gemüse, Obst und Getreide aus der Region, saisonal und aus biologischem Anbau – haben zahlreiche Vorteile: gesündere Ernährung durch weniger Fett und Eiweiß, keine Aufnahme von Pestiziden, Antibiotika und unerwünschten Hormonen mit der Nahrung, intensiverer Geschmack sonnengereifter Früchte, weniger Tierleid. Die Böden können sich regenerieren, mehr CO_2 sowie Wasser speichern und die Biodiversität verbessern, was größere Widerstandsfähigkeit gegen negative Klimaeffekte sowie verlässlichere landwirtschaftliche Erträge zum Vorteil der Bauern bedeutet. Gleichzeitig stellt der Humusaufbau eine der wichtigsten Maßnahmen im Kampf gegen den Klimawandel dar. Veränderungen der Kleidungs- und Freizeitgewohnheiten, Gebäudeadaptierungen sowie Anpassungen in vielen anderen Bereichen bringen zahlreiche weitere Vorteile. Eine Schlüsselrolle spielt dabei die Abkehr von einem ökonomischen System, dessen Stabilität auf Wachstum

beruht und dessen erklärtes Ziel die Gewinnmaximierung ist; das dazu tendiert, alles in Geld zu messen und von Fragmentierungen und Skaleneffekten zu profitieren; das individuell optimierten Lösungen einen maximalen Nutzen für die Gesellschaft als Ganzes zuschreibt.[9] Von ähnlich großer Bedeutung ist der Umbau unseres Finanz- und Währungssystems, das die Realwirtschaft um ein Vielfaches übersteigt und dessen Regeln dafür sorgen, dass Wohlstand und Einkommen systematisch von den Armen zu den Reichen umverteilt werden.[10]

Fazit: In den Industriestaaten dominiert nach wie vor die Welt, wie wir sie kennen, die Welt des Überflusses; gleichzeitig spüren viele Menschen bereits die Auswirkungen jenes verhängnisvollen Szenarios, das uns erwartet, wenn wir die Entwicklung nicht überdenken und rasch korrigieren. Die Wissenschaftler*innen sind aufgerufen, ihren Elfenbeinturm zu verlassen und sich dem gemeinsamen Kampf für eine Zukunft anzuschließen, die sich durch völlig andere und weitaus sinnvollere Formen des Überflusses auszeichnet.

1—Meadows, Dennis / Meadows, Donella / Zahn, Erich / Milling, Peter (1972) *Die Grenzen des Wachstums. Bericht des Club of Rome zur Lage der Menschheit.* München: Deutsche Verlags-Anstalt.
Raworth, K. (2018) *Die Donut-Ökonomie. Endlich ein Wirtschaftsmodell, das den Planeten nicht zerstört.* München: Hanser.
2—Spratt, D. / Dunlop, I. (2018) *What lies Beneath. The Understatement Of Existential Climate Risk.* Breakthrough.
3—Rockström, J. / Steffen, W. et al. (2009) A safe operating space for humanity. In: *Nature,* 461, 472.
Steffen, W. / Richardson, Katherine / Rockström, Johan et al. (2015) Planetary boundaries: Guiding human development on a changing planet. In: *Science* 349, 1286–1287.
Steffen, W. / Rockström, J. et al. (2018) *Trajectories of the Earth System in the Anthropocene. Proceedings of the National Academy of Sciences.*
4—Daly, H. (1992) Vom Wirtschaften in einer leeren Welt zum Wirtschaften in einer vollen Welt. In: Goodland / Daly / Serafy / Droste (Hg.) *Nach dem Brundtland-Bericht: Umweltverträgliche Wirtschaftliche Entwicklung.* Bonn: Rheinischer Landwirtschaftsverlag.
Daly, H. (2015) *Economics for a Full World.* The Great Transition Initiative.
5—IPCC (2014) *Klimaänderung 2014:* Synthesebericht. Beitrag der Arbeitsgruppen I, II und III zum Fünften Sachstandsbericht des Zwischenstaatlichen Ausschusses für Klimaänderungen (IPCC) [Hauptautoren, R. K. Pachauri und L. A. Meyer (Hg.)]. IPCC, Genf, Schweiz.
6—Steininger, K. / König, Martin / Bednar-Friedl, Birgit / Kranzl, Lukas / Loibl, Wolfgang / Prettenthaler, Franz (2014) *Economic Evaluation of Climate Change Impacts. Development of a Cross-Sectoral Framework and Results for Austria,* Heidelberg New York Dordrecht London: Springer.

7—Weizsäcker, E. U. v. / Wijkman, A. et al. (2018) *Come On! Capitalism, Short-termism, Population and the Destruction of the Planet. A Report to the Club of Rome.* New York: Springer Science.
8—APCC (2018) Österreichischer Special Report Gesundheit, Demographie und Klimawandel, Austrian Special Report 2018 (ASR18), Vorabdruck. In: (APCC), A. P. O. C. C. (Hg.). Wien, Österreich.
9—Raworth, K. (2018) *Die Donut-Ökonomie. Endlich ein Wirtschafts-modell, das den Planeten nicht zerstört.* München: Hanser.
10—Lietaer, Bernard / Arnsperger, Christian / Goerner, Sally / Brunnhuber, Stefan (2013) *Geld und Nachhaltigkeit: Von einem überholten Finanzsystem zu einem monetären Ökosystem. Ein Bericht des Club of Rome, EU-Chapter.*

BRIEFING FOR AFTER ABUNDANCE

CONTEXT

According to the Austrian Climate Change Assessment Report, the impact of increased temperatures has been greater in Austria as a result of its landlocked position, relatively high altitude, and sensitive Alpine regions. Without increased efforts to adapt to climate change, Austria's vulnerability will increase, particularly in areas such as agriculture, forestry, and winter tourism. The shape and form of daily life in Austria in this not-so-distant future will be determined by water shortages, intense and frequent droughts, heatwaves, floods, volatility in the price and availability of food, the interruption of import supply chains, greater difficulties in farming and agriculture, lower levels of tourism, economic and political instability, systems failure and damage to infrastructure, and climate refugees.

Today, unless we live close to where these changes are most intense, we have little or no sense of climate change's looming impact on the country. While everyday life, as we know it, will have to undergo rapid changes, it is difficult, often impossible to understand and imagine the consequences of these changes—for our families, friends, homes, and work.

The disconnect between scientific, data-driven predictions and the absence of visible, tangible signs gives rise to cognitive dissonance, leaving implications mostly unspoken, unsettling and ominous. But this is also a space which offers an opportunity to confront our fears and anxieties, experimenting with ways in we can address the shocks and disruptions of climate change. This is where investigative approaches to design can help us imagine possible futures, not always desirable, and respond to urgent challenges.

BRIEF

Based on this context, the brief invited the students to explore and investigate a post-abundant Austria—an Austria that has already transitioned from abundance to scarcity as a consequence of climate change. For now we can buy food from supermarkets whenever we want, or access endless and reliable supplies of energy and water simply by pressing a switch or turning a tap. We challenged the students to imagine instead a different future, one that is frugal, scarce, deeply uncertain, perhaps even chaotic. What will this post-abundant future feel like? The students were asked to explore this future; a time and place where things have changed, often in radical ways, and through their projects to demonstrate what they have done to mitigate the shock and combat uncertainty.

The students were supported in the conceptual framing of this brief by anthropologist Justin Pickard, who accompanied us on the field trip. Our tutors at *Design Investigations* encouraged the students to embrace conceptual and practical rigour in their research and prototyping, ask questions, and be bold and ambitious. The final outcome *After Abundance* reflects this pedagogical rigour and the value of such collaborative, multidisciplinary education.

DAS BRIEFING

FÜR
AFTER
ABUNDANCE

HINTERGRUND

Dem Österreichischen Sachstandsbericht Klimawandel zufolge wirken sich Temperaturerhöhungen in Österreich aufgrund der Binnenlage des Landes sowie seiner vergleichsweise hohen Lage und sensiblen Alpenregionen stärker aus. Ohne zusätzliche Anstrengungen zur Anpassung an den Klimawandel wird sich Österreichs Verwundbarkeit weiter verstärken, insbesondere in Bereichen wie Land- und Forstwirtschaft oder Wintertourismus. In dieser gar nicht so fernen Zukunft werden Faktoren wie Wasserknappheit, schwere Dürren, Hitzewellen, Überschwemmungen, Preisschwankungen und unsichere Verfügbarkeit von Lebensmitteln, Unterbrechungen von Importlieferketten, erschwerte Bedingungen in der Landwirtschaft, Rückgang des Fremdenverkehrs, wirtschaftliche und politische Instabilität, Systemausfälle und Schäden der Infrastruktur sowie Klimaflüchtlinge das Alltagsleben in Österreich prägen.

Wer nicht in unmittelbarer Nähe jener Regionen lebt, die von diesen Veränderungen am stärksten betroffen sind, hat keine oder nur unklare Vorstellungen von den drohenden Auswirkungen des Klimawandels auf Österreich. Zwar wird sich unser Alltagsleben rasant verändern müssen, doch die Folgen dieses Wandels für unser Umfeld – Familie, Freunde,

Zuhause, Arbeit – sind heute nur schwer und nicht selten auch gar nicht fassbar.

Die kognitive Dissonanz, die aus der Kluft zwischen datenbasierten wissenschaftlichen Prognosen einerseits und dem Mangel an konkreten, sichtbaren Anzeichen andererseits resultiert, führt dazu, dass diese Auswirkungen zumeist unausgesprochen, beunruhigend und ominös bleiben. Zugleich bietet diese Situation die Chance, sich den Ängsten und Befürchtungen zu stellen und mit Bewältigungsmöglichkeiten für die drastischen Folgen des Klimawandels zu experimentieren. Hier können investigative Designansätze dazu beitragen, Zukunftsszenarien zu entwerfen (auch wenn diese nicht immer wünschenswert sein mögen) und auf drängende Herausforderungen zu reagieren.

AUFGABENSTELLUNG

Angesichts dieser Tatsachen wurden die Studierenden mit der Aufgabe betraut, sich mit einem Österreich nach dem Ende des Überflusses auseinanderzusetzen – mit einem Land, in dem der Überfluss infolge des Klimawandels bereits der Knappheit gewichen ist. Derzeit können wir unsere Lebensmittel nach Belieben im Supermarkt kaufen und haben zuverlässig und unbeschränkt Zugang zu Energie und Wasser, indem wir einfach einen Knopf drücken

oder den Wasserhahn aufdrehen. Die Studierenden standen vor der Herausforderung, sich eine andere Zukunft vorzustellen: karg, durch Mangel gekennzeichnet, höchst unsicher und vielleicht sogar chaotisch. Wie wird sich diese Zukunft nach dem Ende des Überflusses anfühlen? Ziel war es, eine Zeit und ein Umfeld mit (zum Teil radikal) veränderten Bedingungen zu erforschen und in den einzelnen Projekten Möglichkeiten zur Linderung der Folgen und Bekämpfung der Unsicherheit aufzuzeigen.

Die Studierenden wurden bei der konzeptionellen Gestaltung dieses Schriftsatzes vom Anthropologen Justin Pickard unterstützt, der uns auf der Exkursion begleitete. Unsere Tutoren bei *Design Investigations* ermutigten die Studierenden, konzeptionelle und praktische Strenge in Forschung und Prototyping zu suchen, Fragen zu stellen und mutig und ehrgeizig zu sein. Das Endergebnis *After Abundance* spiegelt diese pädagogische Strenge und den Wert einer solchen kollaborativen, multidisziplinären Ausbildung wider.

FIELD AND WORK

REMIX

Justin Pickard

In August 2018, in the Czech town of Děčín, a prolonged drought reveals something normally submerged beneath the surface of the river Elbe: a *hungerstein* ('hunger stone'). Hailed by the press as one of the oldest hydrological landmarks in central Europe, the boulder is engraved with accounts of hardship from across the centuries, establishing a clear link between low water levels and reduced agricultural yield. The carvings include a warning from 1904: *"If you see me, weep."*

The designers whose work is profiled in this volume started from an understanding that any possible responses to climate change will be local-first, shaped and constrained by existing social institutions and cultural norms. They were tasked with addressing the challenges of distributive justice in a time of managed decline—asking whose voices count, as people are pressed to devise new ways to manage uncertainty and disagreement, and what this might *feel* like, at an emotional level.

To do this, we assumed a broadly anthropological mode of inquiry, starting with a phase of accelerated fieldwork in the Bregenzerwald, in the state of Vorarlberg. This shared experience of a new and unfamiliar landscape, clearly different from our designers' usual home base in the ex-imperial capital of Vienna, but still within the borders of the Austrian nation-state, provided the group with a common reference, an anchor for contrast and comparison. We visited a furniture workshop, stonemason, gravel quarry, two regional museums, and a former hotel temporarily reworked as a creative residency and youth centre. Taking these sites as a point from which to explore how climate change might play out in a recognisably Austrian context, we began to address our "homeblindness"—an obliviousness to those distinctive elements of our own cultural worlds. For the Wiener, the Bregenzerwald was strange, but also familiar.

We encountered an unlikely collapse of space in an exhibition at the Hittisau Women's Museum, a cube of glass and silver fir atop the local volunteer fire station, where a pair of VR goggles transported the viewer from Alpine foothills to the darkened interior of a Maasai *enkaji* (hut), constructed by the tribe's women to accommodate the needs of a community on the move. Treading sphagnum moss and pine needles underfoot, we met with a forester at Sibratsgfäll, who, waving printed graphs and maps, helped us understand the projected impacts of environmental change on the trees surrounding us. We traversed the nearby Georunde, a circuit through a mountain landscape ruptured and remade by a 1999 landslide, and fought to keep ourselves upright in "Felber's crooked house", a building that slid 18 metres downhill, now anchored at a skewed angle—as demonstrated by the spirit level screwed to the wall.

Typically, anthropology concerns itself with the lived present, or recent past, of a particular social setting. With fieldwork experiences still fresh in our minds, shifting from the present to an imagined future, 30-40 years hence, would require a different approach—a tuning or recalibration of attention. In practice, this saw us adopting a logic of *remix,* combining our first-hand observations with news articles, museum exhibits, and found photos. A map of the Roman Empire at its height was pasted alongside an image of a 3D printed gun, a murmuration of starlings, a shaman, a black-and-white photo of a herd of sheep— each representing some aspect or detail of a possible Austria yet-to-come.

Folded in alongside these materials, our designers' fieldwork experiences became fodder for a sustained whole-group process of selection and recombination, finding patterns and tracing connections between seemingly disparate objects, entities, ideas. Running through a volley of accelerated, week-long intermediary design briefs, this remix logic levered open

The geology, topography and climate of the Bregenzerwald in Vorarlberg formed the Alpine, rural learning environment for preparations for *After Abundance.*

the possibility space, helping participants generate new meanings. The big, abstract forces of environmental change were applied to our designers' home towns, as they were asked to localise the challenge, envisioning how climate shifts and resource scarcity might play out differently, not just in Vorarlberg, but in Salzburg, Burgenland, Moscow, or Istanbul. We speculated about repurposed hospitals, new generations of cave-dwellers, monuments printed from beeswax; sketching ways to sonify the weather, simulate absent snowfall, and help

lawmakers empathise with trees. As deadlines drew closer, these rougher, nimbler prototypes ran together—softening at their edges, they became a pool of ideas and resources held in common, with many early ideas, reworked or mutated, making a further appearance in the final projects. One of Austria's network of volunteer fire stations became a convenient front for a black-market cartel. A Tyrolean mask tradition inspired research into Alpine gift-giving rituals, which were, in turn, reimagined as a post-disaster safety net, costumed performers travelling door-to-door, soliciting donations. Church towers became community energy dashboards. Farmers made it rain.

The final outputs of the *After Abundance* project have their seeds in these two contrasting modes of inquiry; *fieldwork and remix.* With one foot in an imagined future, our designers sampled and reworked existing elements of Austrian culture to confront the challenges of climate change, doing so in ways that address enduring anthropological preoccupations with the household, property, production, power, ritual traditions, and how people relate to their natural environment. In this, much like the *hungerstein* of the Elbe, they shine a spotlight on the contingency and frailties of our present moment.

Visits to member workshops of Werkraum Bregenzerwald, from a joinery to a stone quarry, helped participants get to know the regional resources and how they are used.

FELD-FORSCHUNG
UND
REMIX
Justin Pickard

Im August 2018 legte eine lang anhaltende Dürre in der tschechischen Stadt Děčín ein Objekt frei, das gewöhnlich in den Fluten der Elbe verborgen ist: einen *Hungerstein*. Der Felsblock – von der Presse als eines der ältesten hydrologischen Denkmäler Mitteleuropas gefeiert – trägt eine Reihe von Inschriften, die von den Notlagen vergangener Jahrhunderte erzählen; er verknüpft die Niedrigwasserstände des Flusses eindringlich mit verminderten Ernteerträgen. Auch eine Warnung aus dem Jahr 1904 findet sich darunter: *„Wenn Du mich siehst, dann weine."*

Die in diesem Buch vorgestellten Projekte basieren auf der Erkenntnis, dass potenzielle Lösungen für den Klimawandel auf der lokalen Ebene ansetzen und im Rahmen bestehender sozialer Institutionen und kultureller Normen ausformuliert werden müssen. Die Aufgabe der beteiligten Designer*innen bestand darin, Probleme der Verteilungsgerechtigkeit in Zeiten des kontrollierten Rückbaus der Kohle-, Öl- und Gasförderung zu thematisieren: Wessen Stimme zählt, wenn Menschen neue Möglichkeiten im Umgang mit Unsicherheit und unterschiedlichen Meinungen finden müssen, und welche *Gefühle* sind damit verbunden?

Zur Annäherung an diese Fragen wählten wir eine vorwiegend anthropologische Herangehensweise, die von intensiven Feldforschungen im Bregenzerwald in Vorarlberg eingeleitet wurde. Das gemeinschaftliche Erleben einer neuen, fremdartigen Landschaft, die zu Österreich gehört und doch so ganz anders ist als die einstmals imperiale Metropole Wien (der übliche Wirkungsbereich unserer Designer*innen), bot der Gruppe einen gemeinsamen Referenzrahmen, eine Basis für Gegenüberstellungen und Vergleiche. Wir besuchten eine Möbelwerkstatt, einen Steinmetz, eine Kiesgrube, zwei Regionalmuseen sowie ein ehemaliges Hotel, das als Zwischennutzung zu einem Kreativ- und Jugendzentrum umgestaltet worden war. Diese Orte dienten als Ausgangspunkte, um mögliche Folgen des Klimawandels in einem typisch österreichischen Kontext zu untersuchen und unsere „Betriebsblindheit" – das fehlende Bewusstsein für das Unverwechselbare unserer eigenen Kultur – zu thematisieren. Den Wiener Projektteilnehmer*innen erschien der Bregenzerwald fremd und vertraut zugleich.

In einer Ausstellung im Frauenmuseum Hittisau, das gemeinsam mit der örtlichen Freiwilligen Feuerwehr in einem Kubus aus Glas und Weißtanne untergebracht ist, stießen wir auf das Phänomen eines „kollabierenden" Raums: Eine VR-Brille entführte die Besucher*innen von den Ausläufern der Alpen in eine dämmrige Massaihütte *(enkaji)*, errichtet von den Frauen des Stammes für die Bedürfnisse ihrer nomadischen Gemeinschaft. Über Torfmoos und Kiefernnadeln wandernd trafen wir einen Förster bei Sibratsgfäll, der uns mit Diagrammen und Karten in der Hand die prognostizierten Auswirkungen des Klimawandels auf die Bäume ringsum erklärte. Wir erkundeten in der Nähe die „Georunde", einen Rundweg in einer Bergregion, die 1999 von einem Erdrutsch dramatisch umgeformt worden war – und hatten einige Mühe, uns in „Felbers schiefem Haus" aufrecht zu halten. Das Gebäude war damals 18 Meter talwärts gerutscht und befindet sich heute in einer stabilen Schräglage, wie eine Wasserwaage an der Wand beweist.

Die Anthropologie beschäftigt sich üblicherweise mit der Gegenwart oder jüngeren Vergangenheit eines bestimmten sozialen Umfelds. Der Perspektivenwechsel von der Gegenwart hin zu einer imaginierten Zukunft etwa 30 bis 40 Jahre nach unserer Zeit erforderte von uns – wir hatten unsere Feldforschungen noch in frischer Erinnerung – eine andere Herangehensweise: ein Abstimmen beziehungsweise Neukalibrieren unserer Aufmerksamkeit. In der Praxis entschieden wir uns für einen *Remix,* für eine Kombination aus eigenen Beobachtungen und Zeitungsberichten, aus Museumsexponaten und gefundenen Fotos. Eine Karte des Römischen Reichs auf dem Gipfel seiner Macht, daneben das Bild einer Schusswaffe aus dem 3D-Drucker, eine Schwarmformation von Staren, ein Schamane, das Schwarzweißfoto einer Schafherde – all diese Objekte repräsentierten Aspekte oder Details eines möglichen künftigen Österreich.

Zusammen mit diesem Material bildeten die im Feld gesammelten Erfahrungen unserer Designer*innen die Basis eines kontinuierlichen Gruppenprozesses, in dem es um das Auswählen und Neukombinieren von Elementen ging, um das Erkennen von Mustern und das Aufspüren von Verbindungen zwischen vermeintlich verschiedenen Objekten, Entitäten und Ideen. In einer Reihe von intensiven Zwischenbriefings, die jeweils eine Woche in Anspruch nahmen, half uns dieser Zugang, Möglichkeitsräume zu erschließen und neue Bedeutungen zu generieren. Die abstrakten Auswirkungen des ökologischen Wandels im Großen wurden auf die Heimatorte der Designer*innen umgelegt; es galt, die Herausforderung zu lokalisieren und mögliche unterschiedliche Ausprägungen von Klimaveränderung und Ressourcenknappheit darzustellen – nicht nur in Vorarlberg, sondern auch im Burgenland, in Salzburg, Moskau oder Istanbul. Wir dachten über die Umnutzung von Krankenhäusern ebenso nach wie über neue Generationen von Höhlenmenschen und gedruckte Denkmäler aus Bienenwachs; gleichzeitig entwarfen wir Möglichkeiten, um das Wetter in Form von Klängen darzustellen, fehlenden Schneefall zu simulieren und Parlamentsabgeordneten zu helfen, sich in Bäume einzufühlen. Das Herannahen der Abgabetermine führte diese dynamischen, noch etwas vagen

Konzepte zusammen – sie reiften heran und bildeten ein Reservoir an gemeinsamen Ideen und Ressourcen; auch viele frühe Einfälle tauchten in den Abschlussprojekten in veränderter oder überarbeiteter Form wieder auf. Eine Wache der österreichischen Freiwilligen Feuerwehr etwa diente als perfekte Tarnung für ein Schwarzmarktkartell. Ein Maskenbrauch aus Tirol regte Erkundungen zu alpinen Schenktraditionen an, die als Sicherheitsnetz für die Zeit nach der Katastrophe neu gedacht wurden – in Form von verkleideten Darsteller*innen, die von Tür zu Tür zogen und um Gaben baten. Kirchtürme verwandelten sich in Anzeigetafeln für den Energielevel von Gemeinschaften. Landwirt*innen ließen es regnen.

Feldforschung und Remix – diese beiden gegensätzlichen Ansätze prägen die Ergebnisse von *After Abundance*. Bestehende Elemente der österreichischen Kultur wurden von unseren Designer*innen aufgegriffen und mit Blick auf eine imaginierte Zukunft neu gestaltet. Ziel war es, den Herausforderungen des Klimawandels durch eine Auseinandersetzung mit grundsätzlichen anthropologischen Fragen (Hauswesen, Besitz, Produktion, Macht, rituelle Traditionen, Beziehung zwischen Mensch und natürlicher Umwelt) zu begegnen. Damit wirft dieses Projekt – ähnlich wie der *Hungerstein* in der Elbe – ein Schlaglicht auf die Ungewissheiten und Verwundbarkeiten unserer Zeit.

THE DESIGN INVESTIGATIONS PROCESS

Nikolas Heep

Species and civilisations become extinct when they over-specialise. Inbreeding and specialisation always do away with general adaptability. Humans are going to be displaced altogether as a specialist by the computer. Humans themselves are being forced to re-establish, employ, and enjoy their innate *comprehensivity.*

All of the above I quote and paraphrase from Buckminster Fuller's book *Operating Manual for Spaceship Earth.* What he wrote in 1969 still rings true today. He dared us to take on the great challenges of our time by looking at the biggest possible picture—Earth—and design specific actions we can take today. To be *macro-comprehensive* and *micro-incisive.*

The repercussions of climate change will be manifold: environmental, financial, political, social. Automation and artificial intelligence will render whole sectors of work obsolete, yet create new fields of occupation, some of which we have not even thought of yet.

So what kind of design process can help you tackle such a complex world and flourish in it? It needs to be equally intricate, yet robust to support the progress of a project. The approach we take is iterative, non-linear and holistic.

By iterative and non-linear we acknowledge that there is no straight line from A to B in the kind of context mentioned above. The three main categories of our work could be described as *research, design* and *manifestation.* During *research* we gain insights, discover gaps in the story. When *designing* we translate what we have learned into a shape and form that we and our fellow humans can understand on an intellectual and—equally importantly—on an emotional level. *Manifestation* means the actual production of what we have designed, be it a prototype, an exhibition, a film or piece of software. I called them categories of work and not stages because they don't build on each other in a linear way, one leading to the other. We go through these phases multiple times during a project and make the transition between them in both directions. The *manifestation* influences the *research* just as much as the *research* informs the *design.*

To work in a holistic way implies that our students look at the subject at hand from different angles, involving a wide range of techniques and skills.

The figure for this kind of process is not the straight arrow pointing forward and up which is so familiar to us from corporate PowerPoint presentations. Much rather it resembles a three-dimensional spiral of progress, overlapping itself at times, featuring several bifurcations and potential alternative outcomes.

In the following I want to give a few concrete examples of how tools included in our design process had a distinct impact on our projects.

RESEARCH
We encourage our students to not only explore their topic from the safety of their desks but also get in touch with actual experts in relevant fields. The members of *Corn Cartel* extensively interviewed a local geneticist, which opened their eyes to what is technically imaginable and let them have a view without blinders on this emotionally and politically charged subject. If anything, it encouraged them to be even more daring and radical in their proposal.

Conversing with external professionals informs their projects, builds networks for the students' future careers and on a basic level is good for their personal development.

SKETCH
The aforementioned transition from research insight into actual design can be a frightening moment. It is the instant where designers declare themselves. Where an opinion is quite literally formed. Sketching by hand is still the most intuitive and fastest tool to make this leap of faith, to find out whether a topic hits home emotionally, whether it lends itself well to visualisation and develops relevance outside the mind of the designer.

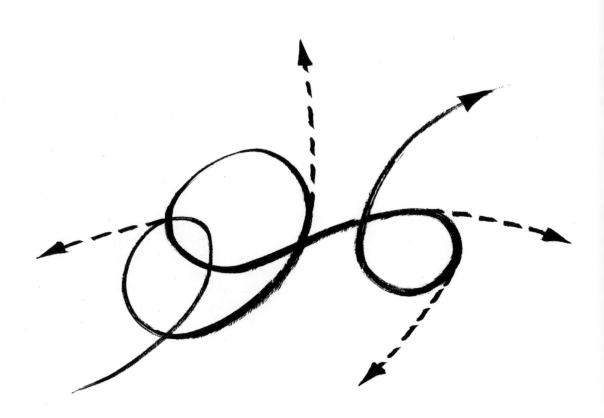

The *Heische* team relentlessly sketched their costumes again and again throughout the entire year. As they pinned up the drawings on the walls around them, their workspace soon became an immersive glimpse of great things to come. The hard part in the end was not to come up with something fitting, but to pick the right designs from many.

MODELS, MOCK-UPS, AND MATERIAL TESTING

Nothing brings an idea to life like a physical mock-up. The true three-dimensionality, the possibility of touching an idea, the chance to place it in different contexts and surroundings are unsurpassed qualities of an analogue model.

The students working on *Illegal Rain* started with a series of scale models of their farmhouse parlour in order to get a feel for their set. They then moved on to testing single elements of the space in 1:1 scale, becoming more realistic and refined with every iteration. Finally they started to build their entire space very early on in our studio in Vienna, giving them the opportunity to fine-tune the design at full scale in a kind of open-heart surgery.

All of the methods mentioned above go hand in hand and are mutually dependent. Every material experiment changes the design, every new design poses new questions, and every new finding influences the story of the entire project. By working through this iterative process, students learn and apply a wide range of skills. They experience that there is more than one side to every story. And we make those stories tangible to everyone through the power of design.

D E S I G N E R
D E S I G N
INVESTIGATIONS
P R O Z E S S

Nikolas Heep

Arten und Zivilisationen sterben durch Überspezialisierung aus. Inzucht und Spezialisierung gehen immer auf Kosten der allgemeinen Anpassungsfähigkeit. Allmählich wird der Mensch insgesamt in seiner Funktion als Spezialist durch den Computer ersetzt. Er selber wird gezwungen, seine schon angeborene *Komprehensivität* anzunehmen, anzuwenden und Freude an ihr zu haben.

Diese einleitenden Worte zitieren und paraphrasieren Gedanken aus Buckminster Fullers 1969 erschienenen Buch *Bedienungsanleitung für das Raumschiff Erde,* das bis heute nichts von seiner Aktualität verloren hat. Fuller forderte auf, uns den bedeutenden Problemen unserer Zeit zu stellen – durch den Blick auf das größtmögliche Ganze, die Erde – und konkrete Maßnahmen zu entwickeln, die im Hier und Heute umsetzbar sind. Er forderte von uns, *makrokomprehensiv* und *mikro-prägnant* zu sein.

Die Auswirkungen des Klimawandels werden vielfältig sein: ökologisch, finanziell, politisch, sozial. Automatisierung und künstliche Intelligenz werden ganze Arbeitsbereiche obsolet machen, doch es werden auch neue Berufsfelder entstehen, von denen wir heute zum Teil noch keine Vorstellung haben.

Welche Art von Designprozess kann uns helfen, es mit einer derart komplexen Welt auf-

zunehmen und sogar in ihr aufzublühen? Er muss vielschichtig und belastbar zugleich sein, um die Fortentwicklung eines Projekts tragen zu können. Der von uns gewählte Ansatz ist iterativ – also auf Wiederholungen beruhend – sowie nicht-linear und holistisch.

Mit *iterativ* und *nicht-linear* erkennen wir an, dass es im oben erwähnten Umfeld keine gerade Linie gibt, die direkt von A nach B führt. Die drei wichtigsten Kategorien unserer Arbeit könnten wie folgt beschrieben werden: *Recherche, Design* und *Realisierung.* Im Rechercheprozess gewinnen wir Einsichten, spüren Lücken in der Geschichte auf. Im *Design* überführen wir das Herausgefundene in eine Form, die wir und unsere Mitmenschen auf intellektueller und – ebenso bedeutend – emotionaler Ebene begreifen können. Mit *Realisierung* ist die tatsächliche Anfertigung des von uns Entworfenen gemeint – sei es als Prototyp, Ausstellung, Film oder Software. Ich spreche von Kategorien und nicht von Stufen, da die drei Bereiche nicht linear aufeinander aufbauen, d.h. nicht von einem zum anderen führen. Wir durchlaufen diese Phasen im Rahmen eines Projekts mehrere Male, und zwar in beide Richtungen. Die *Realisierung* prägt die *Recherche* im selben Maße wie diese in das *Design* einfließt.

Holistisch zu arbeiten bedeutet, dass unsere Studierenden ein Thema aus unterschiedlichen Blickwinkeln betrachten, was ein breites Spektrum an Techniken und Fähigkeiten erfordert.

Diese Art von Prozess lässt sich nicht durch den geraden Pfeil darstellen, der nach rechts oben weist und uns aus den Powerpoint-Präsentationen von Unternehmen so vertraut ist. Er ähnelt vielmehr einer dreidimensionalen Spirale der Entwicklung, die sich an manchen Stellen mit sich selbst kreuzt und durch Verzweigungen und mögliche alternative Ergebnisse gekennzeichnet ist.

Im Folgenden möchte ich anhand einiger Beispiele aufzeigen, wie sich die in unserem Designprozess verwendeten Werkzeuge konkret auf unsere Projekte auswirkten.

RECHERCHE

Wir ermutigten unsere Studierenden, nicht nur vom sicheren Schreibtisch aus die gestellten Themen zu erkunden, sondern mit echten Expert*innen aus relevanten Bereichen Kontakt aufzunehmen. So unterhielten sich die Mitglieder von *Corn Cartel* eingehend mit einem lokalen Genforscher, was ihnen die Augen für das technisch Vorstellbare öffnete und einen unvoreingenommenen Blick auf diese emotional und politisch so brisante Frage erlaubte. Dies bestärkte sie sogar darin, ihren Vorschlag noch kühner und radikaler auszuformulieren.

Die Auseinandersetzung mit Fachleuten von außen prägt die Projekte der Studierenden, schafft Netzwerke für ihre künftige Laufbahn und fördert auf einer sehr grundlegenden Ebene ihre persönliche Entwicklung.

SKIZZE

Der oben beschriebene Schritt von der Forschungserkenntnis hin zum eigentlichen Entwurf kann durchaus beängstigend sein. Dies ist der Moment, in dem die Designer*innen Farbe bekennen müssen, in dem eine Meinung buchstäblich gebildet wird. Das Skizzieren mit der Hand ist noch immer die intuitivste und schnellste Methode für diesen Sprung ins Ungewisse, um herauszufinden, ob ein Thema emotional ankommt, ob es sich zur Veranschaulichung eignet und über die Vorstellungen der Designer*innen hinaus Relevanz hat.

Das *Heische*-Team skizzierte seine Kostüme das ganze Jahr hindurch unermüdlich immer und immer wieder. Die an den Wänden ringsum aufgehängten Zeichnungen verwandelten den Arbeitsbereich der Studierenden rasch in ein immersives Labor vielversprechender Möglichkeiten. Letztendlich bestand die größte Schwierigkeit nicht darin, das Passende zu finden, sondern das Richtige aus so vielen Entwürfen auszuwählen.

MODELLE, MOCK-UPS UND MATERIALEXPERIMENTE

Eine Idee wird am besten mittels Mock-up, also ihrer physischen Nachbildung, veranschaulicht. Die echte Dreidimensionalität, die Möglichkeit, eine Idee zu „begreifen" und in unterschiedliche Kontexte und Umgebungen einzufügen, sind unübertroffene Qualitäten analoger Modelle.

Die Studierenden, die am Projekt *Illegal Rain* mitwirkten, entwickelten zunächst eine Reihe von maßstabsgetreuen Modellen ihrer Bauernstube, um ein Gespür für die Szenerie zu bekommen. Dann erprobten sie einzelne Elemente des Raums im Maßstab 1:1, wobei sie bei jeder Iteration wirklichkeitsgetreuer und differenzierter vorgingen. Schlussendlich bauten sie den gesamten Raum in unserem Wiener Studio bereits sehr früh auf, was eine Feinabstimmung des Designs in Originalgröße gleich einer Operation am offenen Herzen ermöglichte.

Alle hier vorgestellten Methoden gehen Hand in Hand und bedingen sich gegenseitig. Jedes Experiment mit einem bestimmten Material verändert das Design, jedes neue Design wirft neue Fragen auf und jede neue Erkenntnis beeinflusst die Geschichte des gesamten Projekts. In der Auseinandersetzung mit diesem iterativen Prozess erlernen und gebrauchen die Studierenden unterschiedlichste Fähigkeiten. Dabei machen sie die Erfahrung, dass jede Geschichte mehr als nur eine Seite hat. Und wir machen diese Geschichten für jede und jeden greifbar durch die Kraft des Designs.

SCENES OF A LIFE AFTER ABUNDANCE

Led by Anab Jain, 25 students from the University of Applied Arts Vienna's *Design Investigations* (Industrial Design 2) present *After Abundance,* a glimpse of life in a changed rural Austria. Transporting visitors into a world that contends with the stark realities of climate change, the projects in the installation show how those who live in this world face up to new challenges by using tradition and technology, craft and cunning to thrive in an altered landscape.

The five projects in *After Abundance* highlight the importance of systemic thinking, social imagining, critical reflection and multispecies solidarity in design. They were brought to life through objects, stories, film, sound, text, costumes, interactive media and theatrical scenography, demonstrating the designers' interdisciplinary and multimedia approach.

Entering a cosy corner of a rural Austrian home, the patter of falling rain can be heard from one window, while sunlight floods through another. A drone is being assembled on the dining table, with scribbled notes for a chemical recipe lying scattered about. A radio broadcast talks of rogue geoengineering, as sober announcers describe the risks of flooding and drought.

Picking your way through a narrow alley, a pink glow spills through gaps in the planks of a decaying barn, a hint of something brewing behind closed doors. Jostled by costumed locals, dressed as beasts and monsters, you bear witness to the final minutes of their Alpine ritual, as a cacophony of horns, bells, and yelled instructions subsides, giving way to the moaning of wind and cracking of ice. Up ahead, framed by mountains, the face of a melting glacier. Figures clad in white pick their way across the ice, spraying water in a poignant effort to arrest its decline.

SZENEN FÜR EIN LEBEN NACH DEM ÜBERFLUSS

Unter der Leitung von Anab Jain präsentieren fünfundzwanzig Studierende von *Design Investigations* (Industrial Design 2) der Universität für angewandte Kunst in Wien die Installation *After Abundance,* die dem Leben in einem veränderten ländlichen Österreich nachspürt. Die Projekte entführen die Besucher*innen in eine Welt, die mit der düsteren Realität des Klimawandels ringt und in der sich die Menschen mittels Tradition und Technik, Geschick und Findigkeit den neuen Herausforderungen einer veränderten Umwelt stellen.

Die fünf Projekte von *After Abundance* verweisen auf die für den Designprozess wesentliche Bedeutung von systemischem Denken, gesellschaftlichen Visionen, kritischer Reflexion und artübergreifender Solidarität. Sie wurden mit Hilfe von Objekten, Geschichten, Filmen, Klängen, Texten, Kostümen, interaktiven Medien und anderen szenografischen Mitteln zum Leben erweckt und spiegeln den interdisziplinären und multimedialen Zugang der Designer*innen wider.

Besucher*innen, die die heimelige österreichische Bauernstube betreten, werden von Regenprasseln empfangen. Es kommt von einem der Fenster, während ein anderes in helles Sonnenlicht getaucht ist. Auf dem Esstisch eine halb zusammengebaute Drohne, daneben die handschriftlichen Notizen einer chemischen Rezeptur. Eine Radiostimme berichtet von unerlaubten geotechnologischen Maßnahmen und beschreibt in nüchternem Ton die Risiken von Hochwasser und Dürren.

Ein schmaler Zugang gibt den Blick frei auf einen pinkfarbenen Lichtschein, der durch die Bretterfugen eines heruntergekommenen Schuppens dringt – ein Hinweis auf verborgene Aktivitäten hinter verschlossenen Türen. Einheimische, kostümiert als wilde Tiere und Monster, drängen sich zwischen den Besucher*innen, die die letzten Minuten eines alpinen Brauchs miterleben. Eine Kakophonie aus Hörnern, Schellen und gebrüllten Anweisungen weicht dem Heulen von Wind und dem Krachen von Eis. Ein Stück weiter vorne, umrahmt von Bergen, ist ein schmelzender Gletscher zu sehen. Weiß gekleidete Figuren suchen vorsichtig einen Weg über das Eis und versprühen Wasser in dem verzweifelten Bemühen, seinen Rückgang zu stoppen.

ILLEGAL RAIN

"For the first time in forever, it feels like we have reason to be hopeful. The past few months were really dry. The soil turned hard as stone, all the plants suffered, many died. At least the fires have started to burn out.

I'm quite nervous, as this time it'll just be me and my dad. My older brother was caught a few months back, so he is on some police watch list. I hope I don't make any mistakes! My dad always tells me how important it is to be fast, but also precise. So now I have to run to make some illegal rain. Hear you soon."

Anton Rau, 32,
Heische Association Member
and Cabinetmaker

„Zum ersten Mal seit einer Ewigkeit scheint es, als hätten wir Grund zur Hoffnung. In den letzten Monaten war es wirklich trocken. Der Boden war hart wie Stein, alle Pflanzen wurden in Mitleidenschaft gezogen, viele davon sind eingegangen. Zumindest die Brände klingen langsam ab.

Ich bin ziemlich nervös, denn diesmal bin ich mit meinem Vater allein. Mein älterer Bruder wurde vor ein paar Monaten erwischt und steht auf einer Beobachtungsliste der Polizei. Ich hoffe, ich mache keine Fehler! Mein Vater erklärt mir immer, wie wichtig es ist, schnell zu sein, aber auch präzise. Jetzt muss ich aber los, um ein bisschen verbotenen Regen zu machen. Bis bald.“

Anton Rau, 32,
Tischler und Mitglied des
Vereins der Heische

ILLEGAL RAIN BY FLORIAN SEMLITSCH, LUCY LI, AND AGNIESZKA ZAGRABA, OFFERS A PLATFORM FOR DISCUSSING OWNERSHIP OF NATURAL RESOURCES AND CHALLENGES GOVERNMENTS TO DRAFT FAIR LAWS IN THE FUTURE.

Today, water is a public good in Austria. Constitutionally, every Austrian has the right to potable water. No one has to pay for it: like air, water is supposed to be clean and available to everyone. Austria is one of the few countries to have drafted this right into their constitution. Austrians are quite proud of it. The scenario in this project: climate change has radically altered Austria's current reality; water is scarce and regulated.

What if a severe drought hits Austria and the government creates a monopoly on water, including rainfall control, triggering and regulating it through cloud-seeding technology to fall only on state owned farms? What would happen to state-owned farmers?

The first step was to create the broad concept of a water shortage in Austria, creating new realities, value systems, priorities, ideologies, and natural conditions. A bleak scene is painted: permanent droughts and heatwaves have caused natural water reservoirs to almost completely vanish. Land has become impossible to farm. Under these circumstances, the government has taken over the right to rainwater.

What follows is a concrete and intimate narrative, offering a perspective on how this possible future would affect everyday existence—in this case, the lives of farmers in a small village in the Alps. The inability to farm caused by the government's control over rainfall has bred dissatisfaction within the community. Not willing to give up their rural lifestyle and move to the city, like many others, a community of astute farmers has developed strategies to produce their own weather.

Early on in their research, the students discovered cloud-seeding, a process which burns silver iodide with acetone and binds air humidity, generating rain. This is an existing technology, practised by Austria and many other countries to prevent hail. In the fictional scenario here, the government uses this technology to trigger rain on chosen areas. In a twist, however, this same technology is hacked by local farmers in order to produce their own rain and maintain their crops.

When developing the objects and exhibition environment, the students went into great lengths to depict a hyper-realistic scene—a traditional Austrian farmhouse Stube. Every detail of a rural domestic setting was designed to recreate a familiar ambience.

The family home, with its dining table and family portraits, has suspicious and contrasting elements: chemical products on the sideboards, books and diaries with odd notes, a radio broadcasting information on the current governmental system and illegal rain activities, and a huge disassembled drone on the table. A story on the wall and on the headphones completes the narrative.

The central piece of the installation is the weather-hacking drone on the dining table. It is just a prop but scientifically plausible nonetheless. The students researched the technical components of an actual rain-making machine, the amount of silver iodide needed to generate rain effectively and calculated the weight at which their weather-hacking drone would be capable of flying. A reminder that this fictional future is more realistic than we thought.

ILLEGAL RAIN VON FLORIAN SEMLITSCH, LUCY LI UND AGNIESZKA ZAGRABA SETZTE SICH MIT DEN EIGENTUMSRECHTEN AN NATÜRLICHEN RESSOURCEN AUSEINANDER UND APPELLIERT AN DIE REGIERUNGEN, GESETZE IN ZUKUNFT GERECHT ZU GESTALTEN.

Wasser ist heute ein öffentliches Gut in Österreich. Laut Verfassung haben alle Bewohner*innen des Landes ein Anrecht auf Versorgung mit Trinkwasser. Wie auch die Luft soll das Wasser sauber und für alle zugänglich sein. Österreich zählt zu den wenigen Ländern, die dieses Recht in ihre Verfassung aufgenommen haben, und darauf sind die Österreicher*innen sehr stolz. Das Szenario dieses Projekts: eine durch den Klimawandel radikal veränderte Realität, in der das Wasser in Österreich knapp und seine Verfügbarkeit reglementiert ist.

Was wäre, wenn das Land von einer schweren Dürre heimgesucht und die Regierung ein Monopol auf Wasser erheben würde, das auch die Kontrolle der Niederschläge beinhaltet? Wenn der Regen mittels Wolkenimpfung ausgelöst und reguliert würde, so dass ausschließlich landwirtschaftliche Flächen im Staatsbesitz bewässert würden? Was würde aus den heimischen Bauern werden?

In einem ersten Schritt wurde das umfassende Konzept eines durch Wassermangel gekennzeichneten Landes entworfen, mit neuen Realitäten, Wertesystemen, Dringlichkeiten, Ideologien und natürlichen Gegebenheiten. Ein trostloses Bild nahm Gestalt an: Andauernde Dürren und Hitzewellen haben die natürlichen Wasservorräte fast vollständig verschwinden lassen, der Boden kann nicht länger bewirtschaftet werden. In dieser Situation beansprucht die Regierung das Recht auf Regen für sich.

Die Erzählung, die sich daraus entwickelt, zeigt hautnah und unmittelbar, wie sich dieses Zukunftsszenario auf den Alltag auswirken würde, in diesem Fall auf das Leben der Bauern in einem kleinen Alpendorf. Die Tatsache, dass die staatliche Kontrolle über den Regen es unmöglich macht, Landwirtschaft zu betreiben, sorgt für Unmut. Eine Gruppe von findigen Bauern – die nicht bereit ist, ihre bäuerliche Lebensweise aufzugeben und wie viele andere in die Stadt zu ziehen – entwickelt Strategien zur Erzeugung ihres eigenen Wetters.

Bei ihren Recherchen stießen die Studierenden recht schnell auf das Verfahren der Wolkenimpfung, bei dem mittels Verbrennung von Silberiodid-Aceton-Lösungen die Luftfeuchtigkeit gebunden und Niederschlag erzeugt wird. Diese Technik wird in Österreich sowie in vielen anderen Ländern zur Hagelabwehr eingesetzt, während sie im fiktiven Szenario von *After Abundance* der Regierung dazu dient, ausgewählte Gebiete zu beregnen. Doch die heimischen Bauern bemächtigen sich dieser Methode, um selbst Regen für ihre Feldfrüchte zu produzieren.

Bei der Entwicklung der Objekte und des Ausstellungsumfelds setzten die Studierenden alles daran, ein hyperrealistisches Szenario in Form einer traditionellen österreichischen Bauernstube darzustellen: Zur Schaffung dieses vertrauten Ambientes wurde das bäuerliche Wohnumfeld im Detail nachgestellt.

Nicht nur ein Esstisch und diverse Familienporträts zierten die familiäre Kulisse, sondern auch einige verdächtige Elemente, die so gar nicht hierher passten: chemische Substanzen auf der Kredenz, Bücher und Tagebücher mit merkwürdigen Anmerkungen, ein Radio, das über das aktuelle Regierungssystem und Aktivitäten zur Erzeugung von verbotenem Regen informierte, eine riesige zerlegte Drohne auf dem Tisch. Die Geschichte, die mittels Wandtexten sowie über Kopfhörer erzählt wurde, vervollständigte das Bild.

Den Mittelpunkt der Installation bildete die Drohne auf dem Esstisch, die zur Manipulation des Wetters diente. Nur ein Requisit, jedoch wissenschaftlich durchaus überzeugend. Die Studierenden recherchierten die technischen Komponenten einer echten Regenerzeugungsmaschine sowie die Menge des tatsächlich benötigten Silberiodids. Auch das Gewicht wurde genau berechnet, so dass die Drohne flugfähig war – eine Warnung, dass diese fiktive Zukunft realistischer ist als angenommen.

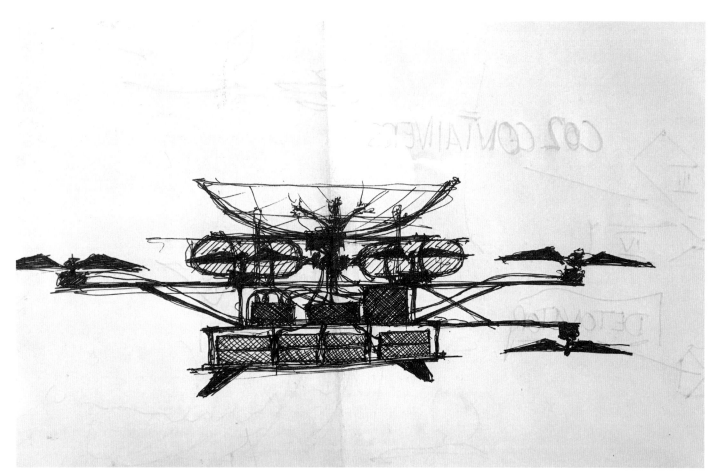

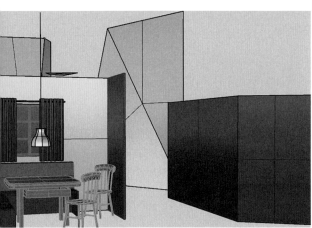

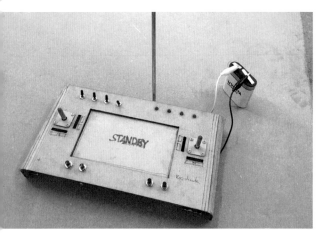

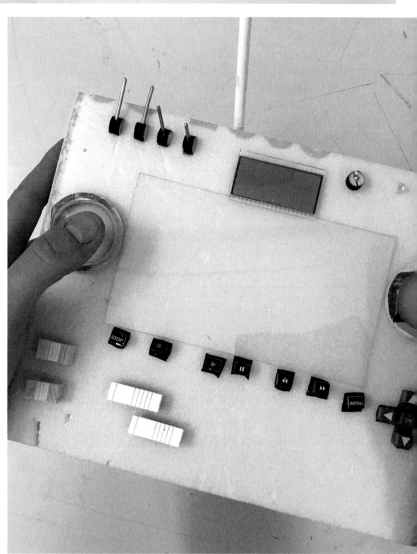

CORN CARTEL

"One of the network nodes broke down today. Only later did I hear some farmer had been arrested, a Vorarlberger. They found his laboratory. I have to admit I'm scared, even though I'm careful when sending out my packages. My own lab here is a stopgap solution, but it does the job. I can document what I'm doing and the steps can be repeated elsewhere. Once again, the companies' PR agencies are all over the news. Anyone who can't afford the correct licences is painted as a villain.

'Unregulated engineering is dangerous', they claim, as if people haven't been moulding and shaping genomes since the dawn of agriculture. Consider corn: from an inedible grass to thousands of varieties, only for 96% of those to be wiped out by the monocropping of big agriculture. We're the ones giving farmers access to real biodiversity."

Anna Moser, 43,
Unemployed

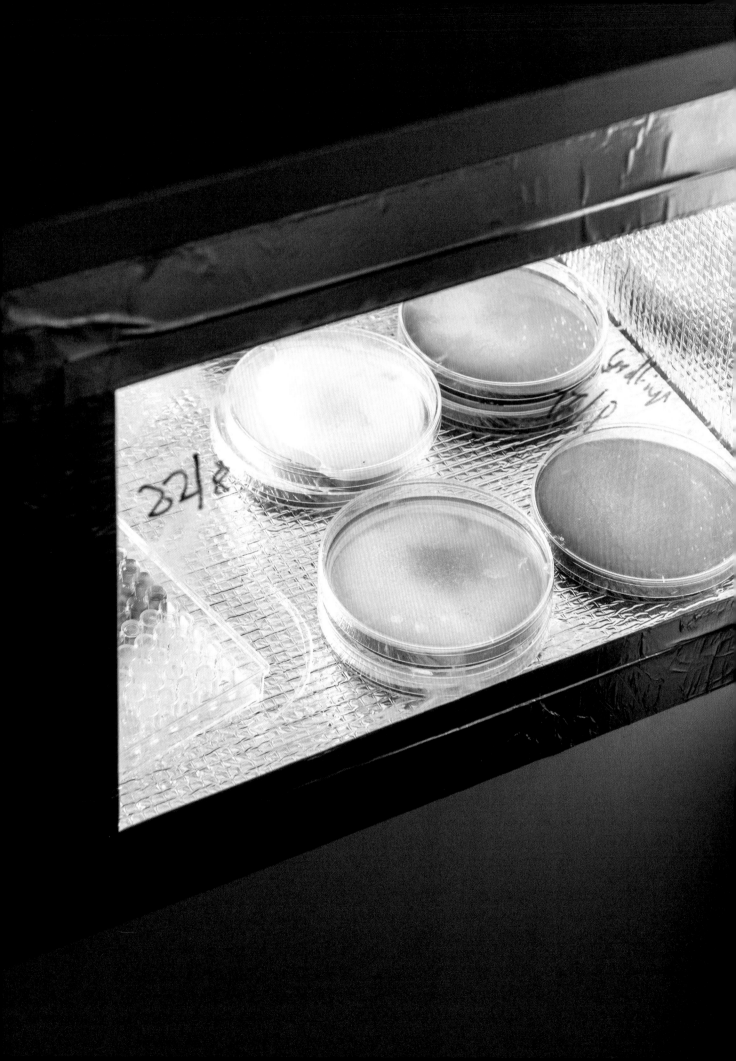

RE-EVALUATE
DE-REGULATE
DISTRIBUTE

„Einer der Netzwerkknoten ist heute aus-
gefallen. Erst später habe ich erfahren,
dass ein Landwirt verhaftet wurde, ein
Vorarlberger. Man hat sein Labor gefunden.
Ich muss gestehen, ich habe Angst,
obwohl ich beim Versenden meiner Pakete
vorsichtig bin. Mein eigenes Labor hier
ist eine Notlösung, erfüllt aber seinen
Zweck. Ich kann dokumentieren, was ich
tue, und die einzelnen Schritte können
andernorts wiederholt werden. Wieder
einmal dominieren die PR-Agenturen der
Firmen die Nachrichten. Wer sich nicht
die richtigen Lizenzen leisten kann, wird
als Schurke hingestellt.
       ‚Unkontrollierte Manipulationen sind
gefährlich‘, heißt es, als hätten die Menschen das Erbgut nicht bereits seit
Anbeginn der Landwirtschaft gestaltet
und geprägt. Denken wir nur an den Mais:
vom ungenießbarem Gras bis zu tausen-
den von Sorten, von denen 96 % durch
die Monokulturen der industriellen Landwirtschaft wieder vernichtet werden.
Wir sind es, die den Bauern Zugang zu
echter Biodiversität verschaffen."

Anna Moser, 43,
arbeitslos

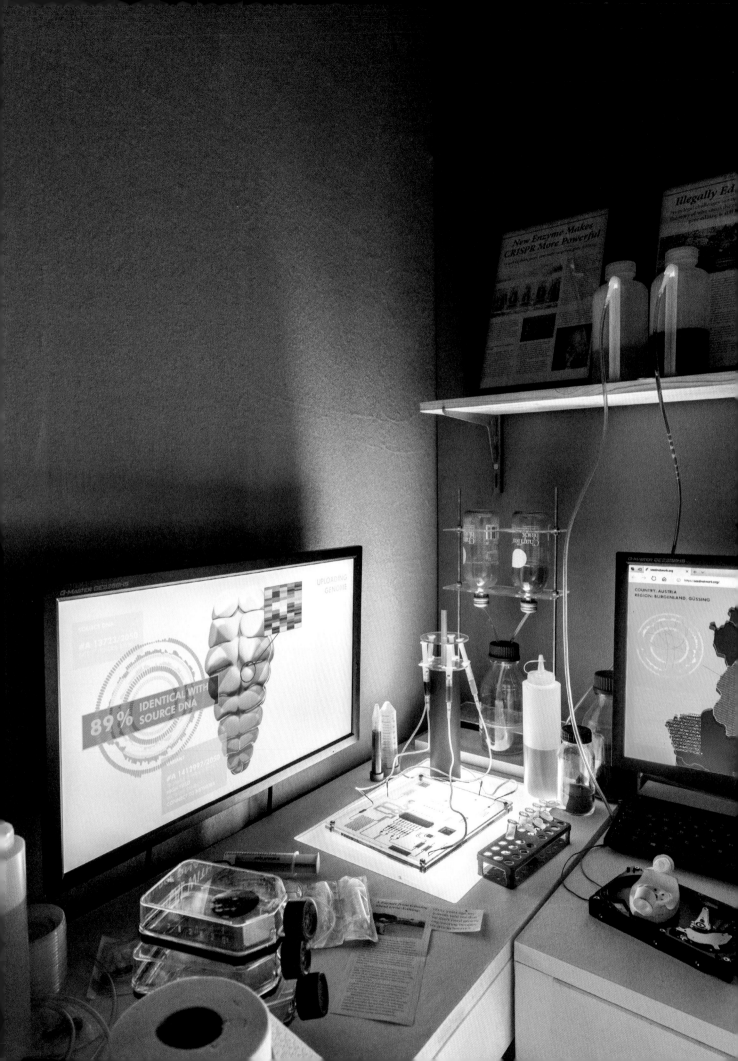

CORN CARTEL, BY SARAH FRANZL, BERNHARD POPPE, JULIA BRANDL, AND ISABEL PRADE, PROVIDES GLIMPSES INTO BIOTECHNOLOGY HACKS, POTENTIALLY MAKING US RE-EVALUATE OUR ETHICAL AND MORAL POSITIONS TOWARDS GENETIC ENGINEERING.

Considering a threatened future, where we would have limited access to resources including food, the group's first question concerned black markets and informal economies. "What would be worth selling in a impoverished future?"

To begin the process, the students explored various different scenarios and realised that in an unstable climate, as the risk of natural disasters increases, food supply might become precarious. How would people ensure they had enough to eat? To start their narrative, the group imagined a character who would then become the protagonist of their story: Anna Moser, a retired biotechnologist who would hoard crops and run a black-market business from her cellar.

Once the nature of the story was established, the students needed to evaluate the plausibility of the fictional narrative. What kind of objects and environment should they design to convey the ideas, values, and priorities of this future? Working closely with experts, two bio-hackers and Karin Garber, the head of the Open Lab in Vienna, a specialist in the legal and practical aspects of CRISPR and an eloquent science communicator, the students learned about genetic engineering, seed hacking, and the ethical problems surrounding our crop and seed distribution.

The controversy surrounding genetic engineering, especially within the context of climate change, is multifaceted. The latest innovation in genome engineering technology was broadly adopted ten years ago: CRISPR, better known as the "gene scissor". Depending on who

you ask, the proliferation of CRISPR will either lead to a world of plenty or disaster of global scale. Austria will be faced with a decision: either to reform agricultural practices, or to risk disruption when local monocultures have difficulty coping with the stress created by extreme weather events.

What if DIY gene editing could increase the stability of crops? Could a kind of seed piracy experiment be developed in opposition to the monopoly of large corporations? This would need to be performed by a community who shared knowledge and interests but also formed an organised resistance against the big

corporations. Anna would have to be part of a larger network engaged in creating new, specialised varieties of corn and making these accessible to farmers.

For the exhibition, the students presented the conceptual laboratory of an illegal CRISPR technician. The first full-scale model was built from cardboard and filled with prototypes of laboratory equipment, growing racks, and corn dispensers, which gradually gave way to their finished counterparts. Detailed research informed the design and construction of the space. They discovered how new technological innovations would change laboratory work and concepts such as Labs on a Chip, which are created in microfluidic platforms requiring a whole room of equipment, and offer greater laboratory efficiency through integration. In the second room, the edited seeds grow on racks. Since the room itself is small, the idea was to imply scale by adding mirrors to the walls for an endlessly repeating room of plants.

The seeds in their story were to be smuggled in glass jars covered with a label declaring it to be artificial honey, since real honey would probably be so rare that it would be substituted with corn syrup.

Every detail was painstakingly designed to give visitors a sense of reality within this speculative scenario, including details to personify Anna Moser, her community, and her daily reality: newspaper articles, re-painted book covers, and hundreds of pieces of ersatz corn, meticulously coloured by hand. The hyper-realism used in this exhibition serves to connect design with science in a seamless way, sparking debate about possible (bio)technological futures.

CORN CARTEL, EIN PROJEKT VON SARAH FRANZL, BERNHARD POPPE, JULIA BRANDL UND ISABEL PRADE, GIBT EINBLICKE IN DAS BIOHACKING UND REGT DAZU AN, DIE ETHISCHE UND MORALISCHE HALTUNG ZUR GENTECHNIK ZU ÜBERDENKEN.

In der Auseinandersetzung der Gruppe mit einem prekären Zukunftsszenario, in dem der Zugang zu Ressourcen – auch Nahrungsmitteln – beschränkt ist, tauchte als allererstes die Frage nach Schwarzmärkten und informellen Ökonomien auf: Was könnten die Menschen in einer von Not und Elend geprägten Zukunft verkaufen?

Zunächst erkundeten die Studierenden unterschiedliche Szenarien und erkannten, dass Klimaschwankungen das Risiko für Naturkatastrophen erhöhen und somit auch die Lebensmittelversorgung gefährden. Wie würden die Menschen ihre Versorgung mit Nahrung sicherstellen? Als Ausgangspunkt diente eine von der Gruppe erdachte Person, die sich zur Schlüsselfigur der Geschichte entwickelte: Anna Moser, eine ehemalige Biotechnologin, die Feldfrüchte hortet und in ihrem Keller einen Schwarzmarkt betreibt.

Sobald die Grundzüge der erfundenen Geschichte feststanden, mussten die Studierenden ihre Glaubwürdigkeit bewerten. Welche Objekte, welches Umfeld sollten sie entwerfen, um die Ideen, Werte und Dringlichkeiten dieser Zukunft zu vermitteln? In enger Zusammenarbeit mit Expert*innen – zwei Biohacker*innen sowie Karin Garber, Leiterin des Vienna Open Lab, Spezialistin für die rechtlichen und praktischen Aspekte von CRISPR und wortgewandte Wissenschaftskommunikatorin – informierten sie sich über Gentechnik, Saatgutoptimierung und ethische Probleme rund um unsere Kulturpflanzen und die Verbreitung von Saatgut.

Die Kontroverse über das Thema Gentechnik, insbesondere im Kontext des Klimawandels, ist sehr facettenreich. Die neueste Entwicklung auf dem Gebiet der Genom-Editierung stößt seit zehn Jahren auf breites Interesse: CRISPR, besser bekannt als „Genschere". Wird die Verbreitung dieser Methode eine Welt des Überflusses schaffen oder eine Katastrophe globalen Ausmaßes? Die Antworten variieren je nachdem, wen man mit dieser Frage konfrontiert. Österreich wird eine Entscheidung treffen müssen: Soll es seine Landwirtschaft umstellen oder Ernteausfälle riskieren, die entstehen, wenn heimische Monokulturen mit der Belastung durch extreme Wetterereignisse nicht zu Rande kommen?

Was, wenn die Genom-Editierung im Do-it-yourself-Verfahren die Widerstandsfähigkeit von Feldfrüchten verbessern könnte? Würde eine Art Saatgutpiraterie gegen das Monopol großer Konzerne entstehen? Dies wäre nur in einer Gruppe möglich, die nicht nur gemeinsame Kenntnisse und Interessen aufweist, sondern auch in organisierter Form Widerstand gegen diese Konzerne leistet. Anna müsste Teil eines größeren Netzwerks sein, das neue, spezialisierte Maissorten entwickelt und diese den Bauern zur Verfügung stellt.

Die Installation präsentierte das fiktive Labor einer illegalen CRISPR-Expertin. Das erste Modell in Originalgröße bestand aus Pappkarton und umfasste prototypische Laborgeräte, Anzuchtregale sowie Vorrichtungen zur Saatgutausbringung, die Schritt für Schritt durch fertige Exemplare ersetzt wurden. Planung und Bauweise des Labors basierten auf detaillierten Recherchen.

Die Studierenden lernten, dass neue technische Innovationen die Arbeit im Labor verändern würden. Sie entdeckten Konzepte wie das Labor-auf-einem-Chip, das auf mikrofluidischen Plattformen basiert und einen ganzen Raum voller Geräte benötigt, die Laborarbeit durch das integrierte Verfahren jedoch effizienter macht. Die behandelten Samen wuchsen auf Regalen in einem zweiten Raum heran. Aufgrund seiner geringen Größe entstand die Idee, ihn mit Wandspiegeln optisch zu erweitern und einen sich endlos wiederholenden Raum voller Pflanzen zu schaffen.

Das Saatgut sollte in Gläsern geschmuggelt und als künstlicher Honig etikettiert werden, da echter Honig aufgrund seiner Knappheit vermutlich durch Maissirup ersetzt werden würde.

Alle Details wurden sorgfältig gestaltet, um den Besucher*innen trotz des spekulativen Szenarios einen Eindruck von Realität zu vermitteln. Dazu gehörten detaillierte Informationen rund um Anna Moser, ihre Gruppe und ihren Alltag: Zeitungsartikel, übermalte Bucheinbände sowie hunderte Maiskornimitate, die die Studierenden sorgfältig von Hand einfärbten. Der Hyperrealismus dieser Inszenierung diente dazu, Design und Wissenschaft nahtlos miteinander zu verbinden und eine Auseinandersetzung mit möglichen (bio)technologischen Zukunftsszenarien anzustoßen.

"Sweat from every pore, gasping for breath, a stabbing in my back—the costume pulling me to the ground. A flash of standing knee-deep in mud, stacking sandbags day and night.

Of stumbling through a burning forest, hoping for survivors lost inside the wads of smoke. A sudden cheering— the heavy bells at our waists fall silent. People press close to me, pulling the mask from my head. My friends' faces are also uncovered, one after another. Our crowd hails us as heroes. They fill our pockets, overwhelming us with their donations. All across the country people await our aid, the spoils from this most ancient of Alpine traditions. Hopeless eyes everywhere. No stories to comfort us, no leaders to lie to us, nothing. Where government failed, the Heische take over. And so our procession moves on."

Anton Rau, 32,
Heische Association Member

„Schweiß bricht aus allen Poren, Ringen nach Luft, ein stechender Schmerz im Rücken – das Kostüm drückt mich zu Boden. Ein Bild schießt mir durch den Kopf: Wir stehen in knietiefem Morast, stapeln Sandsäcke auf, Tag und Nacht.

Stolpern durch einen brennenden Wald, auf Überlebende hoffend, die sich in den Rauchschwaden verirrt haben. Plötzlich Jubel – die schweren Glocken an unserer Taille verstummen. Menschen drängen sich an mich, reißen mir die Maske vom Kopf. Auch die Gesichter meiner Freunde werden nacheinander entblößt. Die Menge feiert uns als Helden. Sie füllt unsere Taschen, überhäuft uns mit Gaben. Im ganzen Land warten die Menschen auf unsere Hilfe, die Ausbeute dieser uralten alpinen Tradition. Hoffnungslose Gesichter allerorten. Keine Erzählungen, die uns aufmuntern, keine Führer, die uns belügen, nichts. Wo die Regierung versagt, übernimmt die Heische. Und so zieht unsere Prozession weiter.“

Anton Rau, 32,
Tischler und Mitglied des
Vereins der Heische

INSPIRED BY TRADITION AND CULTURAL BEHAVIOUR RATHER THAN TECHNOLOGY, *THE HEISCHE* IS A DESIGN EXPERIMENT BY FABIO HOFER, ALI KEREM ATALAY, CATHERINE HU, AND CATALINA GOMEZ ALVAREZ WHICH COMBINES SPECULATIVE DESIGN, CRAFTS, AND TRADITIONS TO RECLAIM SOCIAL BALANCE.

The tradition of "heischen", deriving from the old German word for begging, can be traced back millennia to its pagan roots relating to the alpine goddess "Perchta". Having survived aggressive Christianisation through adaptation, its legacy among cultures spans from Bulgaria to Switzerland. Although its names and rituals diversified, the struggle that gave birth to this tradition was universal: winter.

As an unavoidable and brutal force, winter was thought to be a work of evil. And since humans tend to latch onto superstitions when they feel powerless against certain threats, a tradition to scare away the evil spirits of winter emerged. Interestingly, this tradition was not purely spiritual—it had a concrete aspect in the collection of charitable gifts for those in need. It served as a tool of communal survival by social balancing. Nowadays, in times of luxury and convenience, this tradition has become a mere tourist attraction.

This group's scenario explored the idea that, in a place devastated by climate change, social inequalities would increase. Having discovered the wonderful and ingenious alpine traditions of "heischen", they began to wonder: what if we could redesign this ritual?

Just as the Heische of the past were a reaction to harsh winters, the project concept of post-abundance Austria began with the students' awareness that people would have to endure the brutal forces of nature, facing calamity and despair.

With this in mind, the students carried out in-depth research into their subject. Topics ranged from anthropology to religious rituals, from costume design to material testing. The first challenge was to strip down the traditional Heische ritual to its core elements, such as superstitions, the community-serving aspects of charity and distribution, the religious undertones, characters, and the handcrafted nature behind its costumes and choreography. From these, a framework was established in order to redesign a familiar ritual.

The students elaborated on the costumes with references to natural disasters, searched for materials, and created characters to embody the story, then plotted how would they perform the ritual itself. The characters were personifications of the catastrophes. Each costume was made of debris salvaged from the corresponding disaster, meaning that they could vary regionally, according to how each area was affected. Following the old tradition, the new Heische ritual consists of costumed individuals who travel from door to door in the community, performing a choreography, bringing blessings and collecting donations that are later redistributed among the victims.

The biggest challenge was to design the costumes for the performance, a task accomplished under the mentorship of textile expert and artist Ute Neuber, who is

also a lecturer at the University of Applied Arts. The main concept behind the costumes was to create "non-humanising" figures for the ritual's new characters: the catastrophes.

The project's narrative is intricate and layered. The original Heische costumes anonymised wearers for a reason—nobody knew who would need help the next time. Asking for help is usually shameful, and associated with begging. Within this narrative, however, it was a tremendous honour to be visited by the Heische, as a visit from them meant that the other villagers esteemed this abundant household.

The installation consisted of three life-sized costumes, mounted on structures as if someone were wearing them, and representing wildfire, drought, and flood. Every aspect of the costume was carefully crafted, from the way the structure moved through to the choice of materials that best reflected each disaster. For example, for the 'Drought' character, dried corn was used—a thematic connection to the *Corn Cartel,* another project in the exhibition. Each of the five projects in the exhibition is connected to the others. The inclusion of design or story elements from other projects is a clever way to connect the exhibits as a cohesive group of projects.

NICHT TECHNIK, SONDERN TRADITIONEN UND KULTURELLE VERHALTENSWEISEN INSPIRIERT DAS DESIGNEXPERIMENT VON FABIO HOFER, ALI KEREM ATALAY, CATHERINE HU UND CATALINA GOMEZ ALVAREZ. *THE HEISCHE* VERKNÜPFT SPEKULATIVES DESIGN, HANDWERK UND TRADITIONEN MIT DEM ZIEL, DAS SOZIALE GLEICHGEWICHT WIEDERHERZUSTELLEN.

Die Tradition des Heischens (mittelhochdeutsch für „fordern, fragen") lässt sich über Jahrtausende hinweg bis zu ihren heidnischen Wurzeln rund um die alpine Sagengestalt der Frau Percht zurückverfolgen. Sie widerstand der aggressiven Christianisierung durch Anpassung, so dass sich ihr kulturelles Vermächtnis heute von Bulgarien bis in die Schweiz findet. Die einzelnen Bezeichnungen und Bräuche unterscheiden sich, verdanken ihren Ursprung jedoch ein und demselben Kampf – dem Überleben im Winter.

Der Winter mit seiner unentrinnbaren brutalen Kraft galt einst als Werk des Bösen. Da die Menschen zur Flucht in den Aberglauben neigen, wenn sie sich einer Bedrohung hilflos ausgeliefert fühlen, entstand der Brauch, die bösen Geister des Winters zu vertreiben. Dieser war interessanterweise nicht ausschließlich spirituell begründet: Ein durchaus handfester Aspekt galt dem Sammeln von Gaben für Bedürftige. Die Tradition diente dazu, das Überleben der Gemeinschaft durch sozialen Ausgleich sicherzustellen. Heute, in unserer von Luxus und Komfort geprägten Zeit, ist daraus eine bloße Touristenattraktion geworden.

Das Szenario der Gruppe thematisierte die Idee, dass in einem vom Klimawandel verwüsteten Umfeld die soziale Ungleichheit zunehmen würde.

Nachdem die Studierenden auf das ebenso großartige wie einfallsreiche Konzept der alpinen Heischebräuche gestoßen waren, fragten sie sich: Was wäre, wenn wir dieses Brauchtum neu gestalten könnten?

So wie die Heischetraditionen der Vergangenheit eine Reaktion auf den strengen Winter waren, so entwickelten die Studierenden ihr Projekt aus der Vorstellung heraus, dass die Menschen in einem Österreich nach dem Überfluss den brutalen Kräften der Natur und damit der Not und Verzweiflung ausgesetzt sein würden.

Davon ausgehend untersuchten sie unterschiedlichste Aspekte dieses Themas – von der Anthropologie bis zu religiösen Bräuchen, von der Kostümbildnerei bis zur Materialprüfung. Die erste Herausforderung bestand darin, die zentralen Elemente der traditionellen Heischebräuche herauszuarbeiten (Aberglaube, dem Gemeinwohl dienende Aspekte des Spendens und Verteilens, religiöse Bedeutungen, Figuren, die Handarbeit hinter den Kostümen und Abläufen etc.), um ein System zur Neugestaltung dieser bekannten Tradition zu entwickeln.

Die Studierenden erarbeiteten die Kostüme, die an Naturkatastrophen erinnerten, mit großer Sorgfalt. Sie suchten nach Materialien, schufen Figuren, die ihre Geschichte verkörperten, und überlegten dann, wie sie den Brauch selbst durchführen würden. Die einzelnen Figuren standen für unterschiedliche Naturkatastrophen. Jedes Kostüm war aus Überresten des dazugehörigen Unglücks gefertigt, so dass es regionale Unterschiede gab, je nachdem, in welcher Form das Gebiet betroffen war. In Anlehnung an die alte Tradition zogen kostümierte Personen von Tür zu Tür und vollzogen ein einstudiertes Ritual; sie brachten Segen und sammelten Gaben,

die anschließend unter den Leidtragenden verteilt wurden.

Die größte Schwierigkeit bestand darin, die Kostüme für die Aufführung zu gestalten. Diese Aufgabe meisterten die Studierenden unter Anleitung der Textilexpertin und Künstlerin Ute Neuber, die auch an der Universität für angewandte Kunst Wien unterrichtet. Die wichtigste Idee hinter den Kostümen: Die neu kreierten Figuren des Brauchs – die verschiedenen Katastrophen – sollten nicht „vermenschlicht" werden.

Die Erzählung dieses Projekts war komplex und vielschichtig, die Heischekostüme gaben die Identität ihrer Träger*innen aus gutem Grund nicht preis: Niemand konnte wissen, wer das nächste Mal Hilfe benötigen würde. Während das Bitten um Hilfe üblicherweise als beschämend empfunden und mit Betteln assoziiert wird, galt der Besuch der Heische in diesem Projekt als außerordentliche Ehre. Er bedeutete, dass die Dorfbewohner*innen diesen Haushalt und Überfluss schätzten.

Die Installation bestand aus drei lebensgroßen Kostümen, die auf Gerüste montiert wurden und wirkten, als würden sie gerade getragen werden. Sie standen für Waldbrand, Dürre und Überschwemmung. Alle Details waren sorgfältig gearbeitet, von der Art, wie sich die Konstruktion bewegte, bis zur Wahl der Materialien, um die jeweilige Katastrophe bestmöglich darzustellen. Für die Figur der „Dürre" wurde etwa getrockneter Mais verwendet – ein thematischer Bezug zum *Corn Cartel,* das ebenfalls Teil der Spekulation war. Alle fünf Projekte sollten miteinander verknüpft sein. Die Einbindung von Gestaltungs- und Erzählelementen aus anderen Projekten diente dabei als geschickte Möglichkeit, die Installation als zusammenhängende Erzählung zu präsentieren.

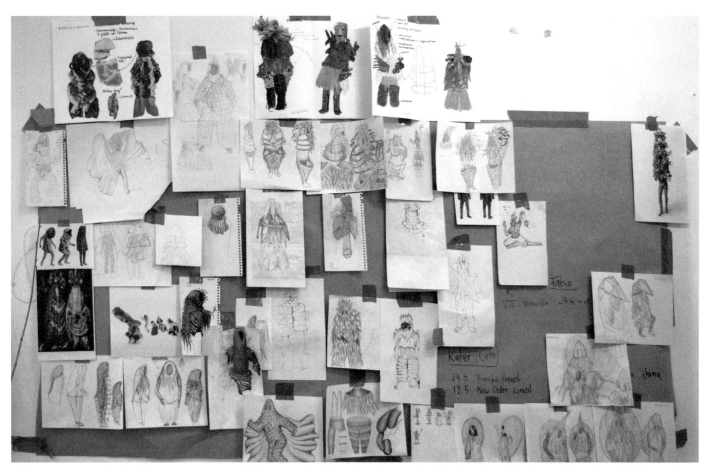

MICROGRID

CHARGING STATION

WEATHER: SU

CHARGING STATION

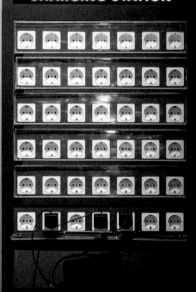

Energy Sharing & Transmission

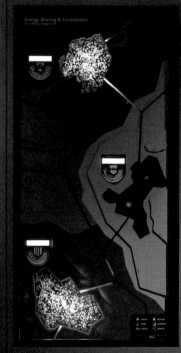

Hierarchical Energy Distribution

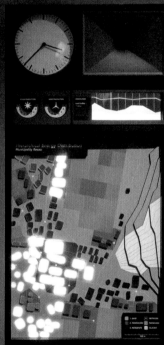

"Things got pretty bad back then. Can you imagine living without power for a week, a month? Providers making excuses and stalling, unable to tell us when things might return to normal? They never did. Eventually, we decided to do something about it. At first, it was just me and a neighbour. A few solar panels on rooftops, a cluster of small wind turbines close to the fields. Later, as more people joined in, we dammed the stream and installed a half-dozen reclaimed power units in an outbuilding down at the farm. It would have been impossible to power everything at once, but with the technology in place, we could begin directing electricity to where it was needed most. Still, it may be better this way. Last year, we connected another village to our grid, and started sharing on a bigger scale. Our final goal is still a way off, but we might yet be able to claw our way back to where we started."

Laura Felder, 53,
Councillor

ivilian Generators

SOLAR PRODUCTION

0
5
10
15
20
25
30
35
40
10x kWh

WIND PRODUCTION

0
5
10
15
20
25
30
35
40
10x kWh

Energy Fo

PRODUCTIO

Load Profile

1. Base

2. Produce

3. Reside

Shortages

ierarchical Energy Distribution

unicipality Bezau

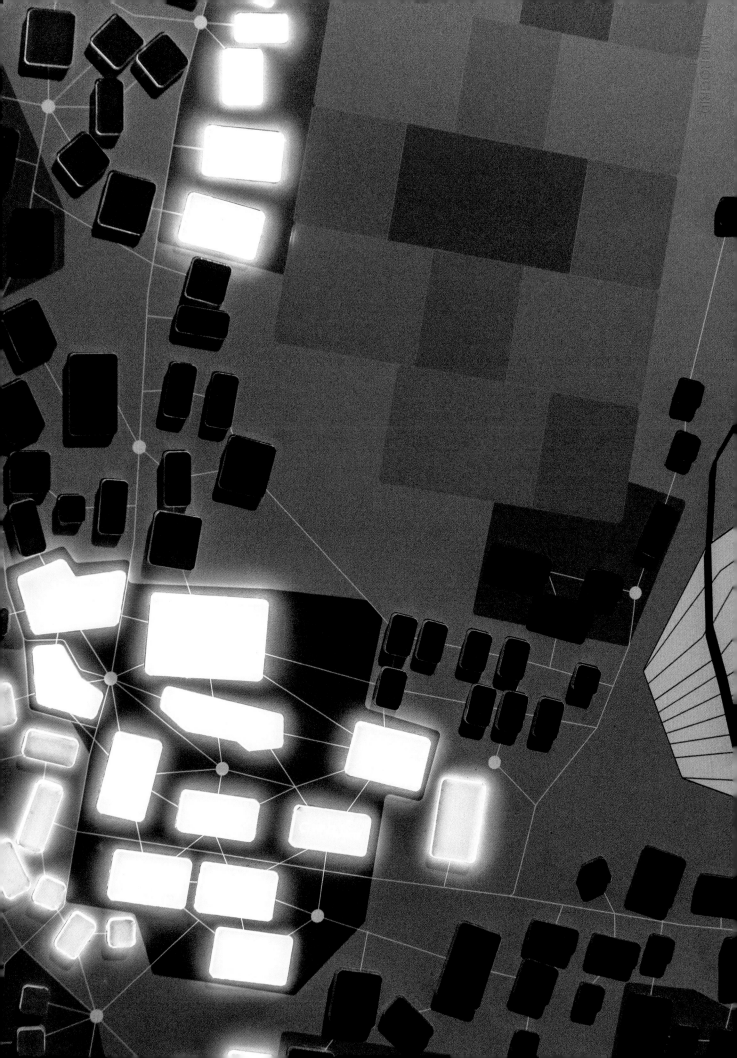

„Die Lage war ziemlich schlimm damals.
Kannst du dir vorstellen, eine Woche, einen
Monat ohne Strom zu leben? Lieferanten,
die sich herausreden und ausweichen,
die nicht sagen können, wann sich die Dinge
wieder normalisieren werden? Zu dieser
Normalisierung kam es nie. Schließlich
beschlossen wir, etwas zu unternehmen.
Zunächst nur ich und ein Nachbar. Ein
paar Sonnenkollektoren auf dem Dach,
eine Ansammlung kleiner Windkraftanlagen
in der Nähe der Felder. Später, als mehr
Menschen mitmachten, stauten wir
den Bach auf und installierten ein halbes
Dutzend gebrauchter Generatoren in
einem Nebengebäude unten am Hof.
Es wäre nicht möglich gewesen, alles sofort
mit Strom zu versorgen, aber mit den nun
verfügbaren technischen Mitteln konnten
wir anfangen ihn dorthin zu bringen,
wo er am dringendsten benötigt wurde.
Vielleicht ist es besser so. Letztes
Jahr wurde ein anderes Dorf ans Netz
angeschlossen und wir begannen, Strom
in größerem Umfang mit anderen zu teilen.
Wir sind noch immer ein gutes Stück
von unserem eigentlichen Ziel entfernt,
doch wir könnten es schaffen und uns auf
den ursprünglichen Stand zurückkämpfen.“

Laura Felder, 53,
Gemeinderätin

CHARGING STATION

ENERGY

Energy Sharing & Transmission
Vorarlberg, Region 3-6

SOLAR PRODUCTION   WIND PRODUCTION

PRODUCTION
Load Profiles:
1. Base

Hierarchical Energy Distribution
Municipality Bezau

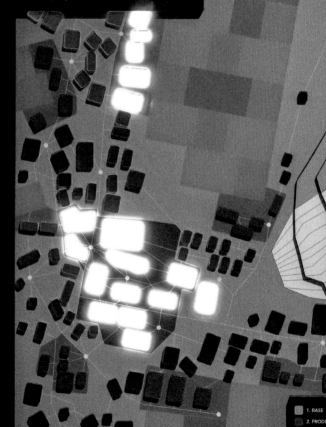

Municipality Bezau

☀ SOLAR   ◆ BIOFUEL

⊥ WIND   REGIONS

1. BASE

2. PRODU

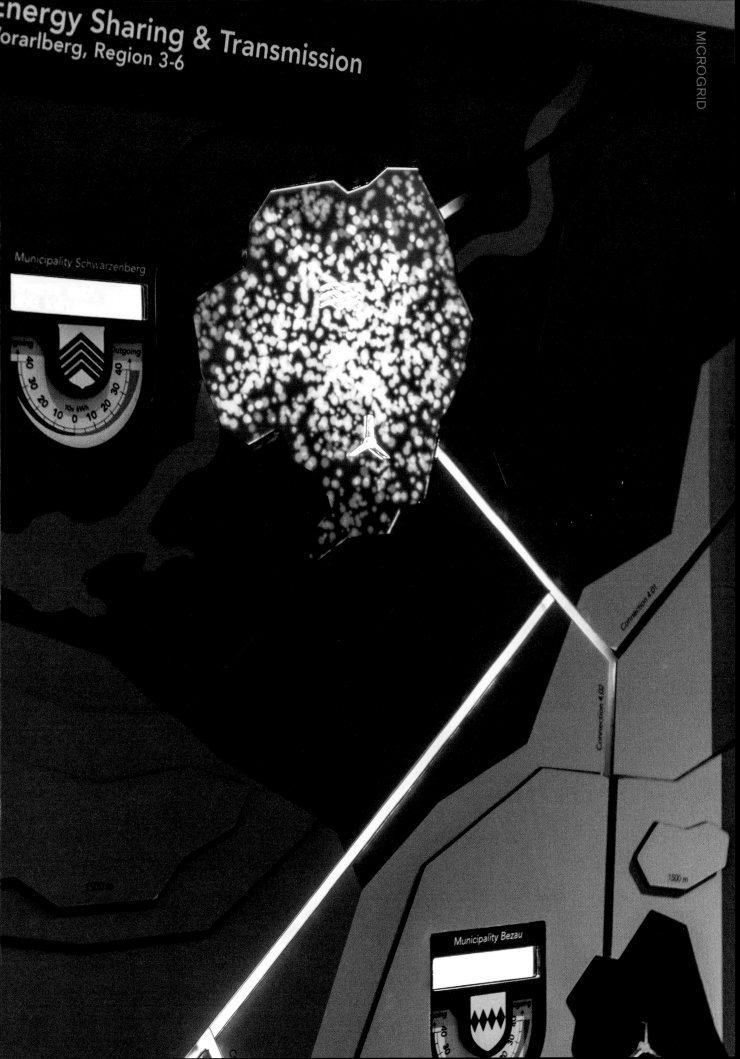

Energy Sharing & Transmission
Vorarlberg, Region 3-6

Municipality Schwarzenberg

Municipality Bezau

Connection 4.01

Connection 4.02

SOLAR PRODUCTION

WIND PRODUCTION

Energy Fore

PRODUCTION

Load Profiles:

1. Base
2. Producers
3. Residents

Hierarchical Energy Distribution
Municipality Bezau

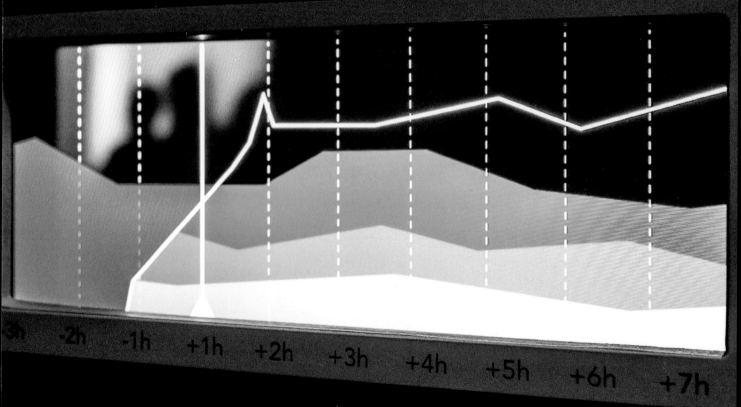

-3h   -2h   -1h   +1h   +2h   +3h   +4h   +5h   +6h   +7h

Municipality Bezau

Municipality Mellau

SOLAR   BIOFUEL

WIND   REGIONS

HYDRO   DENSITY

THE *MICROGRID* PROJECT, DESIGNED BY MAXIMILIAN SCHEIDL, SILVIO SKARWAN, LISI SHARP, SIMON PLATZGUMMER AND MIA MEUSBURGER, EXAMINES ONE OF THE MOST TANGIBLE CONTEMPORARY ANXIETIES ABOUT THE POTENTIAL DAMAGE CAUSED BY CLIMATE CHANGE: THAT ENERGY SYSTEMS COULD BREAK DOWN.

What if energy distribution were to become erratic, and electricity a luxury good? Our society is so dependent on electricity that we cannot really imagine life without it. The Internet depends on it. What if it were no longer so easy to plug and unplug your devices in to charge, to keep servers on? What would happen in hospitals? If you had to choose what to charge, what would you prioritise? Your phones and computers, your fridge to keep food fresh, or your washing machine? How about mobility, with electric cars becoming the next tech invention to save the environment—would they have no functionality without energy? What would we do without a reliable source and distribution of energy?

These and other questions framed the larger scenario of the *Microgrid* group. Once they had decided which approach to take, a short story was created to illustrate the problem. Conventional energy distribution has started to fail. Austrian villages have sought energy autonomy, and formed the *Microgrid:* a local network connecting private and public renewable energy generators, sharing electricity between municipalities to create a more stable power supply in volatile weather conditions. The idea was to take the energy supply into a community's own hands. Villages would be connected through a microgrid, where they could use their own generators to supply the grid and source energy from other small villages around the Alps in cases of necessity. A collective, hands-on and local way to tackle the challenges of energy volatility.

Before starting to design their objects, the students searched for scientific evidence to support their idea. They discovered that many Austrian energy providers offer 100% renewable sources, and that the town of Guessing in Burgenland is the centre of renewable energy in Europe. Energy research is so advanced in Austria that it might enable Vorarlberg, the alpine region where *Design Investigations* conducted their first round of research for the entire project, to become energy autonomous by 2050.

In their research concerning energy in Austria, the group also found geography played a role in energy production. For example, a town on a mountain would be

excellent for wind turbines, yet if one moves a couple of kilometres away into a valley, water turbines offer a better renewable energy source for a village. In other words, if one source collapses when hit by a catastrophe, the other one could back it up. The plausibility of the design speculations is what makes them effective. These design experiments are not intended as cinematic props—they are meant to be believable. In this way, we could imagine ourselves in these scenarios in the very near future.

When developing the objects for the exhibition, students faced the challenge of how to make this complex story visible, since we are hardly aware of the myriad of cables and towers, plugs and sockets that make up today's energy grid. In moments of crisis, one of the most important resources is trustworthy information. Consider hiking trails in Austria—one's first stop is the information stand, with maps, altitude information, difficulty levels for the different trails, emergency phone numbers, and so on.

Inspired by these trailhead information points, the students reimagined the info-stand to display updated information on the upcoming energy shortages or excess production, distribution, and transmission on the microgrid.

The construction of the info-stand involved MDF cutting, LED panel programming, an accurately designed map, and a charging station that would serve as a last-resort power supply during blackouts. The stand functions like a well on the village's main square—where in the past people would have gathered to fetch water, but can now collect electricity during harsh times.

The *Microgrid* info-stand conveys a sense of unity in the exhibition. Besides maps, LED text messages, and a charging station, there is an official radio broadcast reporting on a storm and giving insight into the other stories within the space— an overarching voice that links all the projects.

DAS VON MAXIMILIAN SCHEIDL, SILVIO SKARWAN, LISI SHARP, SIMON PLATZGUMMER UND MIA MEUSBURGER GESTALTETE PROJEKT *MICROGRID* WIRFT EIN SCHLAGLICHT AUF EINES DER AM MEISTEN GEFÜRCHTETEN PROBLEME UNSERER ZEIT, DAS DER KLIMAWANDEL AUSLÖSEN KÖNNTE: AUF DEN ZUSAMMENBRUCH DER ENERGIEVERSORGUNG.

Was würde geschehen, wenn die Energieversorgung immer wieder ausfällt und elektrischer Strom zu einem Luxusgut wird? Unsere Gesellschaft ist so abhängig von Elektrizität, dass wir uns ein Leben ohne sie gar nicht vorstellen können. Ohne Strom gäbe es kein Internet. Was wäre, wenn wir unsere Geräte nicht einfach anstecken könnten, um sie aufzuladen, um einen Server zu betreiben? Was würde mit unseren Krankenhäusern geschehen? Wenn wir wählen müssten, welches Gerät würden wir ans Stromnetz hängen? Unser Smartphone und unseren Computer, unseren Kühlschrank oder unsere Waschmaschine? Und unsere Mobilität? Elektroautos gelten als neueste technische Errungenschaft zur Rettung der Umwelt,

doch ohne Elektrizität hätten sie keinerlei Nutzen. Was würden wir ohne zuverlässige Energiequelle und -verteilung tun?

Diese und andere Fragen flossen in das Szenario der *Microgrid*-Gruppe ein. Sobald sich die Studierenden auf eine Vorgangsweise geeinigt hatten, entwarfen sie eine kurze Geschichte, um das Problem zu veranschaulichen: Die konventionelle Energieversorgung versagt in zunehmendem Maß. Einige österreichische Gemeinden streben nach Energieautonomie und schließen sich zum *Microgrid* – einem lokalen Netzwerk aus privaten und öffentlichen Energieerzeugern – zusammen. Das *Microgrid* basiert auf erneuerbaren Energiequellen und ermöglicht den Austausch von Elektrizität zwischen den Gemeinden, um die Energiezufuhr auch bei unbeständigen Witterungsverhältnissen sicherzustellen. Dahinter steht die Idee, dass eine Gemeinschaft ihre Energieversorgung selbst in die Hand nimmt. Die Gemeinden sind durch das lokale Netzwerk verbunden und können ihre selbst erzeugte Energie in das System einspeisen sowie im Bedarfsfall Energie aus anderen kleinen Alpendörfern beziehen. Eine

kollektive, praktische und ortsnahe Möglichkeit, die Herausforderungen einer instabilen Energieversorgung zu bewältigen.

Ehe sie sich an die Gestaltung der Objekte machten, recherchierten die Studierenden die wissenschaftlichen Grundlagen ihres Konzepts. Sie entdeckten, dass viele österreichische Lieferanten Energie aus hundertprozentig erneuerbaren Quellen anbieten und dass die burgenländische Stadt Güssing das Zentrum für erneuerbare Energie in Europa ist. Die österreichische Energieforschung ist so hoch entwickelt, dass Vorarlberg – wo *Design Investigations* ihre Recherchen für dieses Projekt startete – bis zum Jahr 2050 energieautonom werden könnte.

Die Nachforschungen zur Energiesituation in Österreich ergaben, dass auch die Geografie eine Rolle in der Energieproduktion spielt. So ist etwa eine Windkraftanlage ideal für eine Berglage, während in einem Tal nur wenige Kilometer weiter Wasserturbinen die beste Möglichkeit darstellen, einen Ort mit erneuerbarer Energie zu versorgen. Fällt also eine Quelle durch eine Katastrophe aus, kann die andere für sie einspringen. Je glaubwürdiger spekulative Designkonzepte sind, desto wirkmächtiger sind sie auch. Die Designexperimente waren nicht als bloße Kulisse gedacht, sie sollten überzeugen. Auf diese Weise konnten wir uns in die einzelnen unmittelbar bevorstehenden Zukunftsszenarien hineinversetzen.

Die Entwicklung der Ausstellungsobjekte stellte die Studierenden vor die schwierige Aufgabe, diese komplexen Zusammenhänge sichtbar zu machen, da wir den unzähligen Kabeln und Leitungsmasten, Steckern und Steckdosen unseres modernen Energienetzes kaum Aufmerksamkeit schenken.

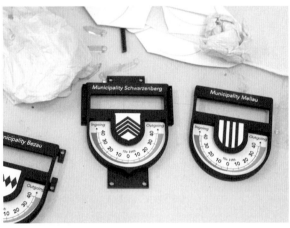

Eine entscheidende Ressource in Zeiten der Krise sind vertrauenswürdige Informationen. Denken wir nur an die österreichischen Wanderwege, deren erste Station aus einem Infostand mit Karten, Höhenangaben, Schwierigkeitsgrad der verschiedenen Wege, Notfallnummern etc. besteht.

Diese Informationspunkte am Beginn von Wanderwegen inspirierten die Studierenden zur Gestaltung eines speziellen Infostands, um aktuelle Daten zu bevorstehenden Engpässen sowie zur Überproduktion, Verteilung und Übertragung von Energie im *Microgrid* anzuzeigen.

Seine Konstruktion erforderte die Konstruktion eines Gehäuses, das Programmieren eines LED-Panels, eine präzise gestaltete Karte sowie eine Ladestation, die im Fall eines Stromausfalls die letzte Möglichkeit zur Stromversorgung darstellen würde. Ähnlich wie der zentral gelegene Dorfbrunnen auf dem Hauptplatz, an dem sich die Menschen einst versammelten, um Wasser zu holen, würde sie in schweren Zeiten Strom bereitstellen.

Der *Microgrid*-Infostand erzeugte das Zentrum der einzelnen Erzählungen der Installation. Neben den Karten, den LED-Textanzeigen und der Ladestation gab es eine offizielle Radiosendung, die über einen Sturm berichtete sowie Einblicke in die Themen der anderen Installationen gab. Eine gemeinsame Stimme, die alle fünf Projekte miteinander verband.

RESTITUTION OF
A GLACIER

"When I was in school, the teacher told us the legend of Gepatschferner, a being so magnificent it bordered three countries. Those who made it to the top spoke of their experiences with awe, but not everyone came back. We also heard stories of mysterious encounters and missing people, the mistakes of those who came before. People treated it with reverence and wonder. Now we are obliged to accord it the same kind of respect. As a kid, I enjoyed the spraying, and it's important that our people are exposed to the practicalities from an early age. It can be dangerous and tiring, particularly in summer, when the meltwater flows can catch you by surprise. Sometimes it feels unfair that our community is tied to this agreement. My family didn't cause this climate shift, but I carry responsibility as a weight on my back."

Johanna Mohr, 39,
Elementary School Teacher

„In der Schule erzählte uns der Lehrer vom sagenhaften Gepatschferner, einem Wesen so mächtig, dass es an drei Länder grenzte. Wer es an seine Spitze schaffte, berichtete mit Ehrfurcht von seinen Erlebnissen, doch nicht alle kehrten zurück. Wir erfuhren auch von geheimnisvollen Begegnungen und vermissten Personen, von den Fehlern unserer Vorfahren. Die Menschen verehrten und bestaunten ihn. Wir müssen ihm heute dieselbe Hochachtung entgegenbringen. Als Kind hat mir das Sprühen Spaß gemacht und es ist wichtig, dass unsere Leute von klein auf mit der Vorgehensweise vertraut werden. Es ist mitunter gefährlich und anstrengend, besonders im Sommer, wenn man vom abfließenden Schmelzwasser überrascht werden kann. Manchmal scheint es unfair, dass unsere Gemeinschaft an diese Übereinkunft gebunden ist. Meine Familie hat den Klimawandel nicht verursacht, aber ich trage die Verantwortung wie eine Last auf meinen Schultern.“

Johanna Mohr, 39,
Grundschullehrerin

NATURAL ENTITY OF GEPATSCHFERNER

This commemorative tablet marks the attribution of personhood to case 7C147/26 (Gepatschferner, Tyrol, Western Austria) following the court order of March 1, 2026, referring to the Declaration of Rights of Natural Entities in Austria - as enacted by article 4 with explicit reference to article 4 (3).

- -

Excerpt of the Declaration of Rights for Natural Entities:

Article 4   Applying Legal Status to a Natural Entity

(1) All Natural Entities have the right to apply for legal status, assuming that they do not hold legal status beforehand. Application for a legal status must be initiated via a petition for a referendum.

(2) Applying legal status to a Natural Entity enables them to obtain the subsequent abilities:

  a. the ability to enforce a claim by legal action

  b. the ability to communicate and interact with other Natural Entities, humans and corporations

  c. the ability to enter and enforce contracts, including smart contracts, with other Natural Entities, humans and corporations

(3) If the Natural Entity cannot enforce its entitled rights by its own capacities and technological means do not sufficiently contribute to the statutory abilities stated in 4 (2b), a guardian acting on behalf of the Natural Entity must be elected in compliance with the regulations of article 10.

(4) The legal corpus of a Natural Entity is not inherently bound to the lifespan of the Entity itself.

Article 5   Inherent Right of All Natural Entities

  a. The right to live in dignity

  b. The right to maintain its identity and integrity as a distinct, self-regulating and interrelated being and to play its role in Austria's Nature for its harmonious functioning

  c. The right to be free from contamination, pollution and toxic or radioactive waste

  d. The right to full and prompt restoration after the violation of the rights recognized in this Declaration caused by human activities

  e. The right to a last will, should full and prompt restoration not be possible and would result in extinction of this Natural Entity [...]

- -

Responsible Guardians: Mag.iur Franz Walser, PD Dr. Andrea Fischer, Dr. Heinz Slupetzky
PD Dr. Andrea Fischer is supervising glacial rebuildig program:

Signed:

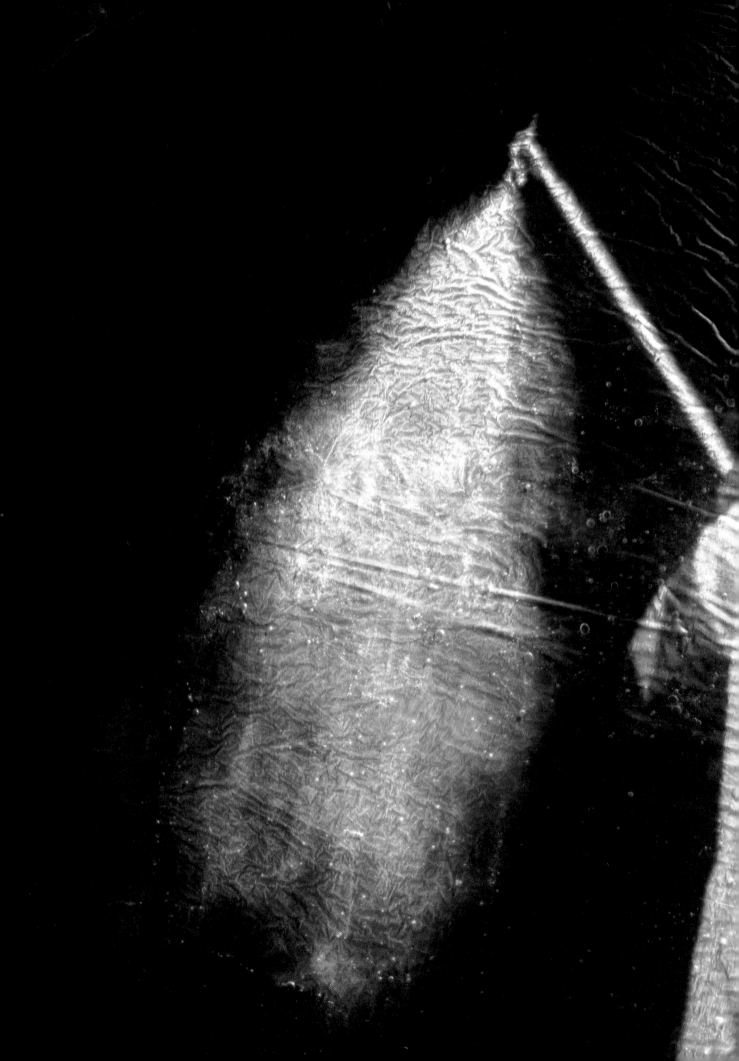

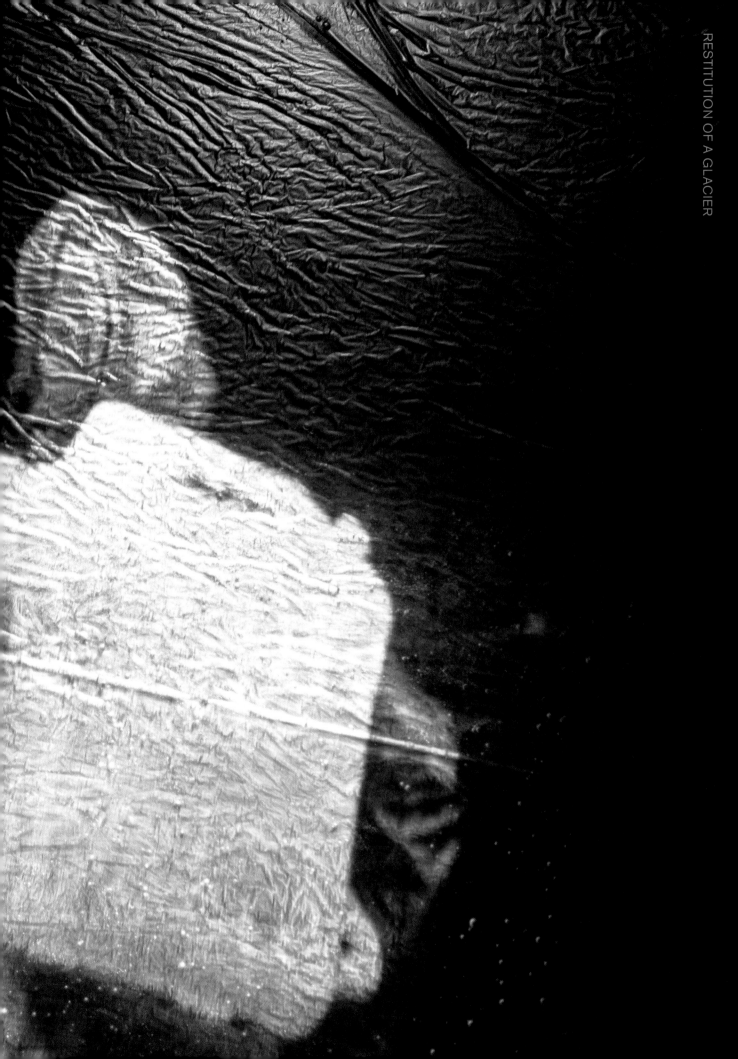

WHAT IF WE HAD TO PAY BACK THE DAMAGE INFLICTED ON NATURE BY THE INCONSIDERATE AND SELF-CENTRED ACTIVITIES OF HUMANS? *RESTITUTION OF A GLACIER* BY SOPHIE FALKEIS, CARMEN FARR, FELIX LENZ, AND ULA REUTINA, INVERTS OUR ASSUMED PERSPECTIVE OF HUMANS AS THE CENTRE OF OUR ECOSYSTEM, MAKING US RETHINK OUR INTERDEPENDENCE WITH NON-HUMAN ENTITIES ON THE PLANET.

We are living in the Anthropocene, the current geological age, viewed as the period during which human activity has been the dominant influence on climate and the environment. Global warming seems to be set in an irreversible motion because of our actions—we are possibly facing ecological catastrophe in the very near future. To protect our planet and therefore ourselves, we urgently need to find ways to develop post-anthropocentric thinking.

The research phase of this project spanned environmental and legal studies. The students were confronted with deep philosophical questions regarding our footprint on Earth—who should be accountable for such injustices, and how? The climate change triggered by global warming will lead to an insurmountable number of problems, impossible for us to fully grasp. During their investigation, they found that global warming, and also glaciers, are regarded as "hyperobjects". These are defined by philosopher Timothy Morton as entities of such vast temporal and spatial dimensions that they defeat traditional ideas about what a thing is in the first place. Hyperobjects have an impact on the way we think, how we coexist, and how we experience our politics, ethics, and everyday existence.

Thinking of history as exclusively human is no longer an option, for the very reason that we are fast-forwarding into mass extinction. One way to reverse this thinking would be to bequest equal status to Nature during human interaction. What if rivers, forests, mountains and oceans were no longer seen as natural resources and instead had legal status, like a person? It seems only logical to grant protection to Nature by treating it as a legal entity. This is the core idea behind this project.

It turns out that this legal mechanism already exists. Over a decade, the rights-of-nature movement has grown from one law adopted in a small community in the US to a movement which has seen countries enact laws, even constitutional protections, recognising the rights of Nature. In 2008, Ecuador became the first country to enshrine the rights of Nature in its constitution. Now, there are rivers in India, New Zealand, Australia, and Colombia with legal status.

The narrative for the project then emerged from this legal research: As a cultural landmark in Austria and as an indicator for climate change worldwide, a glacier was granted legal status. In the state of post-abundance the Gepatschferner glacier in the Tyrolean Alps, once a magnificent being, is melting at a particularly alarming speed, is represented by its guardian. In accordance with the "Declaration of Rights of Natural Entities," drafted by the students, a triumvirate—a board of three officials jointly responsible for the task—would act as the guardian. Consisting of a legal advocate, a political representative, and a glaciologist, the guardian would act on behalf of the entity, to protect its status, health and wellbeing.

The injured entity, the glacier, asserts its legal rights and instigates a court case, accusing the nearby village of lasting damage. The glacier claims restitution in the form of physical rebuilding which will help re-establish its dignity. This Sisyphean task, monitored by the guardian, is expected to last for several generations. Decades after the court case the village, exemplifying our global society, will still be entangled in this act of restitution.

The greatest challenge the group faced was how to bring a glacier into the exhibition space. After a long search for materials and an installation that would convey the idea of a glacier, the students built an abstract geometric structure, in architectonic dimensions, made of translucent polycarbonate sheets, assembled into moulds, a thin layer of epoxy and fibreglass, covered with wrinkled foil, mounted onto a welded metal construction. Visitors to the exhibition experienced a distinctive soundscape of cracking ice, occasionally interrupted by a loud warning signal. At this, the glacier structure came to life with a projection on its translucent face, showing villagers spraying water onto the glacier in response to the alarm.

A simple image for a complex idea, yet effective, as it easily transports the viewer into the situation. The massive installation prompts debate and discussions about our distorted relationship with Nature and how we must urgently change our ways for a better future.

WAS WÄRE, WENN DIE MENSCHEN FÜR ALLE SCHÄDEN EINSTEHEN MÜSSTEN, DIE SIE MIT IHREM UNÜBERLEGTEN, EGOZENTRISCHEN TUN DER NATUR ZUFÜGEN? *RESTITUTION OF A GLACIER* VON SOPHIE FALKEIS, CARMEN FARR, FELIX LENZ UND ULA REUTINA KEHRT DIE PERSPEKTIVE VOM MENSCHEN ALS VERMEINTLICHEM MITTELPUNKT DES ÖKOSYSTEMS UM UND ERINNERT AN DIE WECHSELSEITIGE ABHÄNGIGKEIT, DIE UNS MIT ALLEN NICHT MENSCHLICHEN WESEN DIESES PLANETEN VERBINDET.

Wir leben im geologischen Zeitalter des Anthropozäns, jener Epoche also, in der die Aktivitäten des Menschen den entscheidenden Faktor für die Entwicklung von Klima und Umwelt bilden. Unser Treiben scheint die globale Erwärmung unaufhaltsam in Gang gesetzt zu haben und es ist gut möglich, dass wir bereits in naher Zukunft mit ökologischen Katastrophen konfrontiert sein werden. Um unseren Planeten – und damit auch uns selbst – zu schützen, müssen wir so schnell wie möglich Wege zur Überwindung unseres anthropozentrischen Weltbilds finden.

Die Recherchen zu diesem Projekt erstreckten sich auf ökologische und rechtliche Aspekte. Die Studierenden waren mit weitreichenden philosophischen Fragen rund um unseren ökologischen Fußabdruck konfrontiert. Wer sollte die Verantwortung für diese Ungerechtigkeiten tragen und in welcher Form? Der von der globalen Erwärmung ausgelöste Klimawandel verursacht eine schier unüberwindbare Anzahl an Problemen, deren Ausmaß wir wahrscheinlich gar nicht begreifen können. Bei ihren Nachforschungen entdeckten die Studierenden, dass die globale Erwärmung wie auch beispielsweise Gletscher als „Hyperobjekte" gelten. Dieses vom Philosophen Timothy Morton entwickelte Konzept bezeichnet Phänomene, deren enorme zeitliche und räumliche Dimensionen sich unseren herkömmlichen Vorstellungen vom Wesen der Dinge grundsätzlich entziehen. Hyperobjekte beeinflussen unser Denken, unser Zusammenleben und die Art, wie wir politische und ethische Fragen sowie unseren Alltag erleben.

Die Vorstellung, die Geschichte beschränke sich auf den Menschen, ist nicht länger haltbar, gerade weil wir im Anthropozän ungebremst auf ein Massenaussterben zusteuern. Eine Möglichkeit zur Veränderung dieser Haltung bestünde darin, der Natur einen Status zu verleihen, der sie dem Menschen gleichstellt. Was wäre, wenn Flüsse, Wälder, Berge und Ozeane nicht länger als natürliche Ressourcen betrachtet würden, sondern über einen eigenen Rechtsstatus verfügten, ähnlich wie Personen? Es scheint nur logisch, die Natur zu schützen, indem wir sie zum Rechtssubjekt erklären. Das war die zentrale Idee dieses Projekts.

Wie sich herausstellte, existiert dieses Rechtsinstrument bereits. In den letzten zehn Jahren ist eine Bewegung für die Rechte der Natur entstanden, ausgehend von einem Gesetz in einem kleinen US-amerikanischen Ort bis hin zu ganzen Staaten, die Gesetze über die Rechte der Natur – zum Teil sogar im Verfassungsrang – erlassen haben. Das erste Land, das die Rechte der Natur in seiner Verfassung verankerte, war Ecuador im Jahr 2008. Heute gelten Flüsse in Indien, Neuseeland, Australien und Kolumbien als eigene Rechtspersonen.

Aus diesen juristischen Recherchen entwickelte sich die Geschichte des Projekts. Als Wahrzeichen der österreichischen Kultur und Gradmesser für den Klimawandel weltweit wurde ein Gletscher zum Rechtssubjekt ernannt: In der Zeit nach dem Ende des Überflusses vertritt ein Sachwalter den Gepatschferner, einen ehemals mächtigen Gletscher in den Tiroler Alpen, der in besorgniserregendem Tempo schmilzt. Gemäß der von den Studieren-

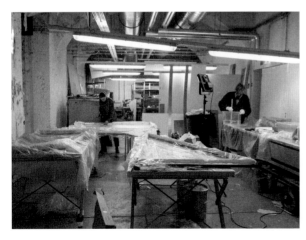

den entworfenen „Deklaration über die Rechte natürlicher Wesen" besteht der Sachwalter aus einem dreiköpfigen Gremium, das gemeinsam für diese Aufgabe verantwortlich zeichnet. Ein*e Rechtsvertreter*in, ein*e Repräsentant*in der Politik und ein*e Glaziolog*in treten im Namen des Gletschers auf, um seinen Status und sein Wohlergehen zu schützen.

Der Geschädigte – der Gletscher – nimmt die ihm zustehenden Rechte in Anspruch und strengt ein Gerichtsverfahren an. Er beschuldigt das nahe gelegene Dorf, ihn dauerhaft geschädigt zu haben, und fordert seine physische Wiederherstellung, um seine Würde wiederzugewinnen. Diese Sisyphusarbeit unter Aufsicht des Sachwalters wird sich vermutlich über viele Generationen erstrecken. Jahrzehnte nach dem Gerichtsverfahren ist das Dorf – das sinnbildlich für die globale

Gesellschaft steht – noch immer mit diesem Akt der Restitution beschäftigt.

Die größte Herausforderung für die Gruppe bestand darin, einen Gletscher in den Ausstellungsraum zu bringen. Um diese Idee vermitteln zu können, war eine aufwändige Suche nach Materialien und Installationskonzepten erforderlich. Schließlich konstruierten die Studierenden eine abstrakte geometrische Struktur architektonischen Ausmaßes, die aus lichtdurchlässigen Polycarbonatplatten bestand. Die Platten wurden mittels einer dünnen Schicht aus Epoxidharz und Fiberglas zusammengefügt, mit geknitterter Folie überzogen und auf eine geschweißte Metallkonstruktion montiert. Die Besucher*innen wurden mit den charakteristischen Geräuschen von krachendem Eis empfangen, gelegentlich unterbrochen durch ein lautes Warnsignal. In diesen Momenten erwachte das

gletscherartige Gebilde zum Leben: Eine Projektion auf die durchscheinende Oberfläche der riesigen Konstruktion zeigte Dorfbewohner*innen, die den Gletscher auf das Alarmsignal hin mit Wasser besprühten.

Ein schlichtes, aber wirkmächtiges Bild für eine komplexe Idee, das ein unmittelbares Erleben der Situation ermöglichte. Die wuchtige Installation thematisierte nicht nur unsere verzerrte Beziehung zur Natur, sondern zeigte auch mit großer Dringlichkeit, dass wir uns ändern müssen, um eine bessere Zukunft zu ermöglichen.

DEBRIEFING OF AFTER ABUNDANCE

Stefan Zinell

When asked whether we would like to be the Austrian contributor to the London Design Biennale 2018, we considered it a huge honour. We were to be the first academic department to be part of a show that, up until then, had presented only professional studios.

At the same time, we began an intense and candid internal discussion. Some of our key questions focused on the pedagogic values of such an endeavour. Now, in hindsight, these can be answered more easily than at that moment of making the decision. Including a project like this within our educational framework presented a number of complexities, which I would like to describe here.

A fundamental decision we made very early in the process was that our contribution should represent the ideas and concepts of as many as possible of the students involved. At some moments, it would have been far easier to focus our project on a single, concise message. Such a concept would also have streamlined the development and production process and perhaps made it easier for visitors to the Biennale to understand and interpret our installation. On the other hand, it would have turned some of our students into mere executives responsible for implementing the ideas and concepts of others. We therefore tried to avoid this strategy, and we succeeded in implementing an installation in which many of the students find themselves—a decision that increased the motivation of all involved, and this motivation proved to be essential.

The design, construction and manufacture of our installation was subject to a number of outside parameters. External deadlines, budgets, international security standards and much more can rarely receive enough attention within university education. In addition, we were able to work with a production budget that was well above the standard available. This allowed us to create an installation that we would never have been able to finance

Design Investigations and the Biennale team on a field trip to "Felbers schiefes Haus" and Georunde Rindberg in Sibratsgfäll in the Bregenzerwald, where a landslide devastated an entire village in 1999.

without external support. This further resulted in important learning experiences for our students, who were able to work with materials and equipment that they otherwise often can only simulate or suggest in their university projects. They experienced what it means to go through each phase of a project with consistent precision and rigour.

Added to this was another privilege, namely the dialogue with a broad public. This aspect, the contact with the observers, proved in my opinion to be thoroughly positive. By that I mean less the media attention that our institute, our university or the curator got—although this was also highly appreciated. More interesting for us—from a learning perspective—was the experience of what messages our audience received as we had intended, and which they did not. Since our didactic approach includes a comprehensive and constant monitoring of the progress of our students' projects, we as teachers are thoroughly

familiar with all projects. The resulting proximity inevitably makes it difficult to maintain an objective view. To make up for this we regularly invite guests to presentations, reviews and final exams. These guests, however, come almost exclusively from the creative field. The London Design Biennale, on the other hand, enabled us to connect with a wider and diverse audience and to engage with their impressions and opinions about our installation. The feedback showed, for example, that our show was perceived by some as "darker" and more dystopian than we had intended.

As a university, our job is to encourage students and to explore and challenge the limits of what is possible. To do this we must create a suitable environment in which they can take risks and sometimes even risk failure. The fact that we accepted the challenge and signed a binding contract with outside entities could have influenced our thinking and actions in this regard, as it also reduced the scope for such failure. The importance of this factor is difficult to assess—but we can say with certainty that we did not consciously "play safe".

To sum up, I think that an event of this kind is very useful for a university institution: a great motivation and a valuable external "reality check", whilst also understanding economic and commercial commitments. Therefore I think these engagements should be a kind of regular exception. Ideally, every generation of students should have experienced something similar at least once during their academic education. For a five-year diploma study like ours, this would mean that comparable actions should be carried out approximately every three years. In our field of investigative design, the medium of an exhibition is important vehicle (although not the only) for the communication of our creative and ethical positions. For our graduates, it also becomes a mechanism for furthering their career and funding their practice. So, the opportunity to learn how to deal with the complex and multi-layered aspects of the cultural and creative industries is essential. The more thoroughly they understand the mechanisms involved, the better they will be able to assert themselves in the market and develop their economic and moral positions.

However, projects of this kind also show us the value and significance of our regular semester projects—not being in the spotlight of a Biennial. They make clear to us the privileged environment in which we are allowed to teach and research, and how valuable and important this freedom is.

DIE NACHBESPRECHUNG VON
AFTER ABUNDANCE
Stefan Zinell

Die Einladung, Österreich bei der London Design Biennale 2018 zu vertreten, war eine große Ehre für uns. Als erste universitäre Einrichtung sollten wir an einer Ausstellung teilnehmen, die bis dato professionellen Studios vorbehalten war.

Die Einladung war auch der Beginn einer internen Diskussion, die ebenso intensiv wie offen geführt wurde. Einige der grundlegenden Fragen, die wir uns stellten, drehten sich um den didaktischen Wert eines solchen Unterfangens. Heute, im Rückblick, können manche diese Fragen leichter beantwortet werden als zum Zeitpunkt der Entscheidungsfindung. Die Einbindung eines Projekts dieser Art und Größe in unser Ausbildungskonzept konfrontierte uns mit einer Reihe von komplexen Herausforderungen, die ich im Folgenden darlegen möchte.

Eine grundlegende Entscheidung, die wir sehr früh im Prozess trafen war jene, dass unser Ausstellungsbeitrag die Ideen und Konzepte von möglichst allen beteiligten Studierenden repräsentieren sollte. In manchen Momenten wäre es weitaus einfacher gewesen, unser Projekt auf eine einzige, konzise Botschaft zu fokussieren. Ein solches Konzept hätte auch den Entwicklungs- und Produktionsprozess gestrafft und den Besucher*innen der Biennale vielleicht das Verständnis und die Deutung

unserer Installation erleichtert. Es hätte jedoch andererseits manche unserer Studierenden zu bloßen Ausführenden gemacht, zuständig für die Umsetzung der Ideen und Konzepte anderer. Wir versuchten daher, diese Strategie zu vermeiden, und es gelang uns, einen Beitrag zu realisieren, in dem sich viele der Studierenden wiederfinden – eine Entscheidung, die die Motivation aller Beteiligten erhöhte und diese Motivation erwies sich als essenziell.

Die Planung, die Konstruktion und die Herstellung unserer Installation unterlag einer Reihe von äußeren Parametern. Externe Deadlines, Budgets, internationale Sicherheitsstandards und vieles mehr können sonst in der universitären Ausbildung nur selten genügend Beachtung finden. Zudem konnten wir mit einem Produktionsbudget arbeiten, das deutlich über dem normalerweise zur Verfügung stehenden Rahmen lag. Dies erlaubte uns die Realisierung einer Arbeit, die wir ohne externe Unterstützung niemals hätten finanzieren können. Daraus ergaben sich weitere wichtige Lernerfahrungen für unsere Studierenden, die mit Materialien und Ausstattungen arbeiten konnten, die sie sonst im universitären Umfeld häufig nur simulieren oder andeuten können. Sie erlebten, was es bedeutet, jede einzelne Phase eines Projekts mit gleichbleibender Präzision und Konsequenz zu durchlaufen.

Dazu kam ein weiteres Privileg, nämlich der Dialog mit einem breiten Publikum. Dieser Aspekt, der Kontakt mit den Betrachter*innen, erwies sich meines Erachtens als durch und durch positiv. Damit meine ich weniger die mediale Aufmerksamkeit, die unserem Department, unserer Universität oder dem Kurator zuteil wurde – obwohl wir auch dies sehr zu schätzen wussten. Interessanter war für uns – aus einer Perspektive des Lernens – die Erfahrung, welche Botschaften bei unserem Publikum so ankamen, wie wir es intendiert hatten, und welche nicht. Da unser didaktischer Ansatz eine umfassende und konstante Begleitung der Fortschritte der Projekte unserer Studierenden beinhaltet, sind wir als Lehrende mit allen Arbeiten eingehend vertraut. Die daraus resultierende Nähe erschwert es unweigerlich, einen objektiven Blick zu bewahren. Um dies auszugleichen, laden wir regelmäßig Gäste zu Präsentationen, Rezensionen und Abschlussprüfungen ein. Diese kommen jedoch fast ausschließlich aus dem kreativen Bereich. Die London Design Biennale ermöglichte es uns hingegen, mit einem breiteren und bunt gemischten Publikum in Kontakt zu treten und uns mit dessen Eindrücken und Meinungen über unsere Installation auseinanderzusetzen. Die Rückmeldungen zeigten uns beispielsweise, dass unser Beitrag von manchen Besucher*innen als pessimistischer und dystopischer wahrgenommen wurde, als wir es beabsichtigt hatten.

Als Universität ist es unsere Aufgabe, die Studierenden zu fördern und sie zu ermutigen, die Grenzen des Möglichen zu erforschen und in Frage zu stellen. Dazu müssen wir ein geeignetes Umfeld schaffen, in dem sie auch Risiken eingehen und zuweilen auch scheitern können. Die Tatsache, dass wir die Herausforderung angenommen und einen verbindlichen Vertrag mit einer externen Organisation abgeschlossen hatten, könnte unser diesbezügliches Denken und Handeln beeinflusst haben, denn damit verringerte sich auch der Spielraum für Misserfolge. Die Bedeutung dieses Faktors lässt sich schwer einschätzen – wir können jedoch mit Gewissheit sagen, dass wir nicht bewusst „auf Nummer sicher" gegangen sind.

Zusammenfassend lässt sich meines Erachtens sagen, dass eine Veranstaltung dieses Formats für eine universitäre Einrichtung durchaus von Nutzen ist. Eine große Motivation und ein wertvoller externer „Reality Check" auf der einen Seite, steht einer ökonomischen und kommerziellen Verpflichtung andererseits gegenüber. Daher finde ich, dass solche Engagements als eine Art regelmäßige Ausnahme stattfinden sollten. Idealerweise sollte jede Generation von Studierenden im Zuge ihrer akademischen Ausbildung zumindest einmal etwas Ähnliches erlebt haben. Für ein fünfjähriges Diplomstudium wie unseres würde dies bedeuten, dass vergleichbare Aktionen etwa alle drei Jahre durchgeführt werden sollten. In unserem Fachgebiet der *Design Investigations* hat sich das Format der Ausstellung zu einem wesentlichen Vehikel für die Kommunikation unserer Positionen entwickelt. Für unsere Absolvent*innen bedeutet sie zudem eine wichtige Einkommensquelle – die Möglichkeit, sich mit den komplexen und vielschichtigen Aspekten der Kultur- und Kreativwirtschaft auseinanderzusetzen, ist daher essenziell für die Studierenden. Je gründlicher sie die betreffenden Mechanismen verstehen, desto besser werden sie sich auf dem Markt durchsetzen und ihre Positionen in wirtschaftlicher und moralischer Hinsicht behaupten können.

Projekte dieser Art führen uns aber auch den Wert und die Bedeutung unserer regulären Semesterprojekte vor Augen. Sie machen uns deutlich, in welch privilegiertem Umfeld wir lehren und forschen dürfen und wie wertvoll und wichtig diese Freiheit ist.

E P I L O G U E   O F   A   C L I M A T E   S C I E N T I S T

Kate Marvel

I see the future every day. It lives on my computer screen, in flickering lines of code and terabytes of data written on magnetic tape. I'm a climate scientist, and given the right inputs, I can solve a system of interlocking equations, time step by time step, and tell you exactly what to expect. Physics, after all, is the closest we ever get to magic. Every child learns the alchemy of motion in school: force is the product of mass and acceleration. If we know the strength of the push or pull on a massive object, we can predict its exact path: how it will speed up, and when it will come to rest.

Of course, it's a little more complicated than that. Balls roll cleanly across smooth floors when you push them, but are slowed by the invisible force of friction. The planet, too, is made up of things we understand: water, ice, air, dirt, rock. Perhaps theoretically we could track the motion of every droplet of water and speck of dust, writing untold billions of equations to predict their futures. But we don't have a computer powerful enough to do this, and we never will. We see fragmented glimpses of the future, never its entirety.

The characters in *After Abundance* inhabit these fragments. These projects are speculative stories, but they are deeply experiential. They extend the cold, clinical future that lives inside the computer code of my climate models into visceral, poignant reality. Global warming, after all, affects a particular and special planet. Climate change happens here, in the world we build for it, to the people we know and the children we created.

In *After Abundance,* the planet is a minor character. There is no Mother Earth, just a very large rock. A miraculous rock, to be sure, floating just the right distance from a mediocre star, awash in liquid water and wrapped in the warm embrace of a gaseous atmosphere. But rocks, however wondrous, do not make for interesting characters. They are passively subject to the laws of physics and unmoved by notions of justice. The world is not trying to punish us for our sins. It is not trying to save us, either.

These projects resist the dangerous temptation to reduce climate change to a simple morality tale. It is wrong to assume climate change will compress the spectrum of human emotion into despair, guilt, and resignation. Even on a warming world, people will still experience joy. When the glaciers melt and the forests burn and all the elephants are dead, there will still be love affairs and jokes and minor annoyances. On an Earth ravaged by climate change, the vast majority of humans may never utter the words "climate change". They will blame more immediate causes: food prices, fires, the weather. They will blame each other.

Climate change is simply too big a problem to be left to scientists. It takes expertise to warn, but anyone can imagine. And that is what *After Abundance* invites us to do. Imagine a future populated by people like us, with hopes and dreams and fears. Imagine glaciers come to life as they retreat, granted legal personhood by a grateful populace. Imagine parched earth watered by illegal rain and the genetic guts of staple crops stirred and spliced and rearranged. Imagine my child grown to adulthood, suffering in the world we have made for him. Imagine these things in the hope that they will never come true. And imagine what we can do to prevent them.

Here is what we know about the future: without radical changes to our economy and ways of life, we will continue to put more carbon dioxide into the atmosphere. These molecules will trap the heat radiated by our planet, arresting infrared photons on their journey from the Earth to cold space. With every degree of warming, the atmosphere will hold seven percent more water vapour, which it will drop on us in enormous rainstorms. But it will grow thirstier too, driving increased evaporation from already arid regions. This is the paradox of what is to come: floods and droughts, heat waves and snowstorms, rising seas and retreating glaciers. Climate change will be the biggest story, the increasing note in the background of the planet's discordant symphonies. But it will not be the only story.

We have data and equations, models and theory, but we have no observations of things that have not yet happened. So scientists, like artists and designers, are telling tales about the future. Speculative fiction, if you're generous. Lies, if you're not. But these fictions are familiar to anyone who has ever looked at a baby and imagined the adult she will one day become. We are characters in our own story, writing science fiction in dust and gas smeared on the sky. Our actions doom us to live in a strange new world, alien life on a foreign planet. The future is the story that becomes true, the world into which we send our children. They will never come back.

EPILOG EINER KLIMAWISSENSCHAFTLERIN

Kate Marvel

Ich habe die Zukunft tagtäglich vor Augen – auf dem Computerbildschirm, in Form von flimmernden Softwarebefehlen und Terabytes an gespeicherten Daten. Ich bin Klimawissenschaftlerin und kann – den richtigen Input vorausgesetzt – komplexe Gleichungssysteme lösen und so Schritt für Schritt genau berechnen, welche Entwicklungen uns wann erwarten. Die Physik hat diesbezüglich etwas von Zauberei. Kinder lernen die Alchemie der Bewegung bereits in der Schule: Kraft als Produkt von Masse und Beschleunigung. Ist die Stoß- oder Zugkraft, die auf einen Körper wirkt, bekannt, können wir seinen Weg exakt bestimmen: seine Beschleunigung ebenso wie den Zeitpunkt, an dem er zur Ruhe kommt.

Natürlich ist die Sache etwas komplizierter. Eine angestoßene Kugel rollt ruhig über eine glatte Fläche, wird jedoch von der unsichtbaren Kraft der Reibung gebremst. Auch unser Planet besteht aus Dingen, die wir erklären können: Wasser, Eis, Luft, Erde, Gestein. Theoretisch könnten wir die Bewegung jedes Wassertröpfchens oder Staubkörnchens beschreiben und mit Myriaden von Gleichungen ihre Zukunft berechnen. Doch die Rechnerleistung reicht dafür nicht aus, weder heute noch in Zukunft. Was wir erblicken, sind Bruchstücke des Kommenden, niemals das Gesamtbild.

Es sind diese Bruchstücke, die die Figuren von *After Abundance* bevölkern. Die Projekte erzählen spekulative Geschichten, die zugleich zutiefst erfahrungsbezogen sind. Sie übertragen die unpersönliche, sterile Zukunft aus den Berechnungen meiner Klimamodelle auf die Realität und lassen sie spür- und greifbar werden – die globale Erwärmung betrifft schließlich einen konkreten, ganz besonderen Planeten. Der Klimawandel beeinflusst die Welt, die wir gestalten, die Menschen, die wir kennen, die Kinder, die wir zeugen.

In *After Abundance* spielt der Planet eine Nebenrolle. Mutter Erde gibt es nicht, nur einen riesigen Gesteinsbrocken – der zweifellos erstaunlich ist: in der richtigen Entfernung um einen durchschnittlichen Stern rotierend, mit Unmengen an flüssigem Wasser und eingehüllt in eine wärmende Gasatmosphäre. Doch Gesteinsbrocken, wie wundersam auch immer, sind keine fesselnden Figuren. Sie unterliegen den Gesetzen der Physik und kennen keine Gerechtigkeit. Die Welt versucht weder, uns für unsere Verfehlungen zu bestrafen noch uns zu retten.

Die einzelnen Projekte widerstehen der gefährlichen Versuchung, die Klimaveränderung auf ihren moralischen Aspekt zu reduzieren. Die Vorstellung, der Klimawandel werde das Spektrum menschlicher Emotionen auf Verzweiflung, Schuld und Resignation verengen, ist falsch. Trotz Erderwärmung werden die Menschen Gefühle der Freude erleben. Auch wenn die Gletscher schmelzen, die Wälder brennen und alle Elefanten tot sind, wird es Liebesaffären, Witze und kleine Ärgernisse geben. In einer von Klimaveränderungen verwüsteten Welt werden die meisten das Wort „Klimawandel" vielleicht nie in den Mund nehmen, sondern näher liegende Ursachen wie Nahrungsmittelpreise, Brände und das Wetter verantwortlich machen. Die Menschen werden sich gegenseitig die Schuld geben.

Das Problem des Klimawandels ist einfach zu groß, um es den Wissenschaftler*innen zu überlassen. Für Warnungen braucht es Fachkenntnisse, doch wir alle können uns Dinge vorstellen – und genau dazu laden die Projekte von *After Abundance* ein. Stellen wir uns eine Zukunft vor voller Menschen wie wir, mit Hoffnungen, Träumen und Ängsten. Zurückweichende Gletscher, die lebendig werden, von einer dankbaren Bevölkerung mit eigener Rechtspersönlichkeit ausgestattet. Ausgedörrte Landstriche, die mittels verbotenem Regen bewässert werden, und Feldfrüchte, deren Genome aufgebrochen, gespleißt und umgestaltet werden. Unsere erwachsenen Kinder, die an der Welt leiden, die wir ihnen hinterlassen. Stellen wir uns all diese Dinge vor in der Hoffnung, dass sie nie eintreffen werden. Und denken wir über Möglichkeiten nach, sie zu verhindern.

Was wissen wir über die Zukunft? Ohne einen radikalen Wandel unseres Wirtschaftssystems und unserer Lebensweise wird der CO_2-Gehalt in der Atmosphäre weiter steigen. Die CO_2-Moleküle behindern die Infrarotstrahlung auf ihrem Weg von der Erde ins kalte Weltall, so dass die von der Erde abgestrahlte Wärme nicht entweichen kann. Mit jedem Grad Erwärmung kann die Atmosphäre sieben Prozent mehr Wasserdampf aufnehmen, der in Form von gewaltigen wolkenbruchartigen Stürmen auf den Planeten fällt. Zugleich wird die größere Verdunstung in wasserarmen Regionen die Erde auch trockener machen. Überschwemmungen und Dürren, Hitzewellen und Schneestürme, steigende Meeresspiegel und schmelzende Gletscher – so sieht unsere paradoxe Zukunft aus. Der Klimawandel spielt darin die Hauptrolle, er ist der Grundton, der in der widersprüchlichen Klangkulisse unseres Planeten immer deutlicher vernehmbar wird. Doch er ist nicht die ganze Geschichte.

Wir haben Daten und Gleichungen, Modelle und Theorien, jedoch keine gesicherten Informationen über noch nicht eingetretene Ereignisse. Wie Künstler*innen oder Designer*innen erzählen auch Wissenschaftler*innen Geschichten über die Zukunft, in Form von Spekulationen oder Lügen – je nach Einschätzung. Mutmaßungen dieser Art sind allen vertraut, die jemals ein Baby gesehen und sich vorgestellt haben, zu welchem Menschen es heranwachsen wird. Wir sind Darsteller*innen unserer eigenen Erzählung, Science-Fiction-Autor*innen, die ihre Geschichten mittels Staub und Gas in den Himmel schreiben. Unser Tun verdammt uns dazu, in einer neuen fremdartigen Welt zu leben, wie Außerirdische auf einem fremden Planeten. Die Zukunft ist die Erzählung, die Realität wird, die Welt, in die wir unsere Kinder hinausschicken. Es gibt kein Zurück.

THOMAS GEISLER focuses on his role as curator, researcher and author on contemporary design and everyday culture. He currently is Director of Werkraum Bregenzerwald—an association of craftspeople with its own exhibition building dedicated to contemporary craft, design, and architecture designed by Peter Zumthor. From 2010 to 2016, he was curator and head of the Design Collection at the MAK Vienna. He played a pivotal role in establishing the Victor J. Papanek Foundation at the University of Applied Arts Vienna. He is the co-founder of Vienna Design Week and has curated exhibitions for the Vienna Biennale and the London Design Biennale. As a co-curator he contributed to *Hello, Robot. Design between Human and Machine.* an exhibition by the Vitra Design Museum in collaboration with MAK Vienna and Design Museum Gent. In 2019 he is the curator of BIO26 in Ljubljana and appointed Director of the Kunstgewerbemuseum of the Dresden State Art Collections (SKD).

ANAB JAIN is Professor and Program Leader at the *Design Investigations* department (Industrial Design 2) at the University of Applied Arts Vienna. An award winning designer, filmmaker and futurist, Jain also co-founded the vanguard foresight and design studio Superflux with Jon Ardern, whose clients include the Government of UAE and UK, UNDP, Red Cross, Mozilla, V&A Museum, Microsoft Research, Samsung and Sony. Her work has won awards from Apple Computers Inc., UNESCO, and the UK Government's Innovation Department and has been exhibited at MoMA New York, Vitra Design Museum and the National Museum of China, amongst others. Jain is a TED Fellow, sits on the boards of London School of Economics Media and Humanitarian Innovation Fund, and regularly presents her practice at conferences like TED, Skoll World Forum, MIT Media Lab and Global Design Forum.

HELGA KROMP-KOLB, a trained meteorologist, was a university professor at the University of Natural Resources and Life Sciences (BOKU) from 1995 on and has been an emeritus professor since 2017. As a university teacher and researcher, her emphasis is on environmental meteorology, particularly the spread of pollution in the atmosphere, UV radiation and stratospheric ozone depletion, and—recently, above all—climate change. Her publications include studies on the spread of radioactive substances from Chernobyl and hypothetical accidents in nuclear power plants close to borders, along with methodical and practical work on the regionalisation of GCM climate scenarios in the Alpine region.

JUSTIN PICKARD is a writer and anthropologist based in West Yorkshire, UK. His work focuses on the lived experience of social and technological change, with particular interests in infrastructural systems, cities and urban settings, and experimental research methods.

NIKOLAS HEEP studied architecture at the TU Berlin and AA London. In 2005 he founded the design studio KIM+HEEP with partner Mia Kim. Projects span from commercial product and interior design to conceptual installations, research and teaching. After joining the Angewandte under Ross Lovegrove, he has subsequently taught alongside Hartmut Esslinger, Fiona Raby and Anab Jain. Each era has added a new perspective on what it is we call design, making *Design Investigations* an exciting and multi-faceted place to work and study. As part of the team Nikolas Heep supports students in their main design projects, and also teaches courses such as "Integrated Expert Labs" and "Project Communications".

ALINE LARA REZENDE is a curator, designer, and journalist. Investigating at the interface of contemporary design and culture, she has reported for several international media outlets and worked for big museums across the globe including MoMA New York, The National Art Center Tokyo, Museum of Contemporary Art Tokyo, Sao Paulo Biennale, Vitra Design Museum. She is the co-founder of SALOON Wien, a network for women in the arts. Currently, she is assitant curator together with Thomas Geisler on BIO26, the Ljubiljana Design Biennial.

STEFAN ZINELL studied Industrial Design at the University of Applied Arts Vienna. After graduating he started his own consultancy, working for clients in the fields of interior, furniture and product design, and joined the Angewandte in a teaching capacity. Stefan Zinell has seen the department transform from a traditional material- and crafts-oriented Masterclass, to a product-based industrial design school, into what *Design Investigations* stands for today. Besides giving his own lectures, he supports students in their main projects and is also involved in the strategic development of the department.

KATE MARVEL is a climate scientist and science writer based in New York City. She is an Associate Research Scientist at NASAGoddard Institute for Space Studies and Columbia Engineering's Department of Applied Physics and Mathematics, and writes regularly for *Scientific American* in her column *Hot Planet*.

AUTORINNEN UND AUTOREN

THOMAS GEISLER setzt sich als Kurator, Forscher und Autor mit zeitgenössischem Design und Alltagskultur auseinander. Derzeit ist er Geschäftsführer des Werkraum Bregenzerwald, einer Vereinigung von regionalen Handwerker*innen mit eigenem Ausstellungsgebäude, das zeitgenössischen Entwicklungen in Handwerk, Design und Architektur gewidmet ist und von Peter Zumthor entworfen wurde. Von 2010 bis 2016 war er Kurator und Leiter der Sammlung Design im MAK Wien. Er trug wesentlich zur Gründung der Victor J. Papanek Foundation an der Universität für angewandte Kunst Wien bei, ist Mitbegründer der Vienna Design Week und hat Ausstellungen für die Vienna Biennale und die London Design Biennale kuratiert. Er ist Ko-Kurator von *Hello, Robot. Design between Human and Machine,* einer Ausstellung des Vitra Design Museums in Kooperation mit dem MAK Wien und dem Design Museum Gent. 2019 ist Geisler Kurator der BIO26 in Ljubljana und als Direktor des Kunstgewerbemuseums der Staatlichen Kunstsammlungen Dresden (SKD) berufen.

ANAB JAIN ist Professorin und Leiterin der Abteilung *Design Investigations* (Industrial Design 2) der Universität für angewandte Kunst Wien. Als preisgekrönte Designerin, Filmemacherin und Zukunftsforscherin gründete Jain zusammen mit Jon Ardern das Avantgarde Foresight- und Designstudio Superflux. Zu ihren Kunden zählen die Regierung der Vereinigten Arabischen Emirate und Großbritannien, UNDP, Rotes Kreuz, Mozilla, V & A Museum, Microsoft Research, Samsung und Sony. Ihre Arbeiten wurden von Apple Computers Inc., UNESCO und der Innovationsabteilung der britischen Regierung ausgezeichnet und wurden unter anderem im MoMA New York, im Vitra Design Museum und im National Museum of China ausgestellt. Jain ist TED-Stipendiatin, sitzt im Vorstand des Medien- und humanitären Innovationsfonds der London School of Economics und präsentiert ihre Praxis regelmäßig auf Konferenzen wie TED, Skoll World Forum, MIT Media Lab und Global Design Forum.

HELGA KROMP-KOLB, studierte Meteorologin, war seit 1995 Universitätsprofessorin an der Universität für Bodenkultur, Wien (BOKU) und ist seit 2017 emeritiert. Als Universitätslehrerin und Forscherin liegt ihr Schwerpunkt bei der Umweltmeteorologie, insbesondere Schadstoffausbreitung in der Atmosphäre, UV-Strahlung und stratosphärischer Ozonabbau und – in letzter Zeit primär – Klimawandel. Ihre Publikationen umfassen Studien zur Ausbreitung radioaktiver Substanzen von Tschernobyl und über hypothetische Unfälle in grenznahen Kernkraftwerken ebenso wie methodische und praktische Arbeiten zur Regionalisierung von GCM Klimaszenarien auf den alpinen Raum.

JUSTIN PICKARD lebt als Autor und Anthropologe in West Yorkshire, UK. Er untersucht die Auswirkungen sozialer und technologischer Veränderungen auf die menschliche Erfahrungswelt und beschäftigt sich insbesondere mit Infrastruktursystemen, Städten und urbanen Schauplätzen sowie experimentellen Forschungsmethoden.

NIKOLAS HEEP studierte Architektur an der TU Berlin sowie an der AA London. 2005 gründete er gemeinsam mit Mia Kim das Designstudio KIM+HEEP. Nikolas Heep beschäftigt sich mit Produktdesign, Innenarchitektur, konzeptuellen Installationen, Forschung und Lehre. Er kam unter Ross Lovegrove an die Universität für angewandte Kunst Wien und hat seitdem an der Seite von Hartmut Esslinger, Fiona Raby und Anab Jain unterrichtet. Jede Ära eröffnete neue Perspektiven auf den Designbegriff, was *Design Investigations* zu einem ebenso spannenden wie facettenreichen Umfeld für Arbeit und Studium macht. Als Teil des Teams unterstützt Heep die Studierenden bei großen Designprojekten und unterrichtet Kurse wie „Integrated Expert Labs" und „Project Communications".

ALINE LARA REZENDE ist als Kuratorin, Designerin und Journalistin tätig. Sie erforscht die Schnittstellen zwischen zeitgenössischem Design und Kultur und schreibt für mehrere internationale Medienunternehmen. Arbeit für bedeutende Museen auf der ganzen Welt, darunter das MoMA New York, The National Art Center Tokyo, das Museum of Contemporary Art Tokyo, die Biennale von São Paulo sowie das Vitra Design Museum. Rezende ist Mitbegründerin des SALOON Wien, eines Netzwerks für Frauen der Wiener Kunstszene. 2019 kuratiert sie gemeinsam mit Thomas Geisler die Design Biennale in Ljubljana (BIO 26).

STEFAN ZINELL studierte Industrial Design an der Universität für angewandte Kunst in Wien. Nach Abschluss seines Studiums gründete er ein eigenes Beratungsunternehmen für Innenarchitektur, Möbel- und Produktdesign und begann an der Universität für angewandte Kunst Wien zu unterrichten. Er hat die verschiedenen Entwicklungsphasen des Instituts miterlebt – von der traditionellen Meisterklasse mit ihrem Schwerpunkt auf Material und Handwerk über eine produktorientierte Ausbildungsstätte für Industriedesign bis hin zum zeitgenössischen Konzept der *Design Investigations.* Neben seinen Lehrveranstaltungen unterstützt Zinell die Studierenden bei großen Designprojekten und wirkt an der strategischen Ausrichtung des Instituts mit.

KATE MARVEL arbeitet als Klimawissenschaftlerin und Wissenschaftsjournalistin in New York City. Sie ist Associate Research Scientist am Goddard Institute for Space Studies der NASA sowie am Institut für angewandte Physik und Mathematik an der Columbia Engineering und schreibt in ihrer Kolumne *Hot Planet* regelmäßig für die Zeitschrift *Scientific American.*

ACKNOWLEDGEMENTS

After Abundance, the Austrian entry to the London Design Biennale 2018, is a joint project with many contributors. It is thanks to the far-sightedness of the Federal Chancellery that the significance and importance of Austria participating in this international exhibition of contemporary design was recognised. We would like to extend our particular thanks to the Federal Minister Gernot Blümel and the Arts and Culture Division at the Federal Chancellery, represented by Director General Jürgen Meindl, and to Gudrun Schreiber, Olga Okunev and Gerhard Jagersberger for their trust in inviting us to do the Austrian contribution.

Austria's invitation to take part once again in the London Design Biennale testifies to the appreciation and international recognition of this country's creative output. Biennale President Sir John Sorrel and Artistic Director Dr. Christopher Turner along with the entire team headed by Sumi Ghose were not only full of enthusiasm for *After Abundance,* but also enabled what was a complex and expansive installation in the historical rooms of Somerset House. We would also like to thank mischer'traxler studio (Katharina Mischer and Thomas Traxler), the designers of the Austrian contribution in 2016, for their advise during the initial stages of the exhibition development.

In terms of assistance on site, the Austrian Embassy headed by the Ambassador Dr. Michael Zimmermann and the Austrian Cultural Forum London headed by Katalin-Tünde Huber and her staff Elisabeth Freudensprung, Christa Marchardt, Petra Freimund, Vanessa Fewster, Claudia Ott and Balachandra Arunachalam were important partners and an interface to the Biennale.

The project was also given substantial assistance from the Federal State of Vorarlberg and Vienna. Special thanks are due to the Cultural Department of the Vorarlberg Regional Government headed by Landesrat Dr. Christian Bernhard and the Head of Department Dr. Winfried Nußbaummüller and their team in Bregenz. Thanks to Vorarlberg Tourismus GmbH headed by Christian Schützinger and the support of Gerald März and their team in Dornbirn, it was possible to hold a special information event for international media in collaboration with Austrian National Tourist Office in London. We are also grateful to the Bohlinger + Grohmann company who assisted us with their expertise in structural analysis, making an important contribution to the realisation of the project.

The memorable opening celebration for the Austrian team, official guests, and all new friends of the Biennale attracted particular attention. The event was organised by departure, the creative centre of the Vienna Business Agency headed by Elisabeth Noever-Ginthör, and with the support of Alice Jacubasch and Ute Stadlbauer. The event was further proof of Austria's great hospitality!

An excursion to the Bregenzerwald at the beginning of the project afforded a glimpse of life and work in rural Alpine areas and the challenges and adaptations required by climate change in the region and globally. The trip included a tour of some of the workshops of Werkraum Bregenzerwald, particularly the Tischlerei Mohr (cabinetmaker) and the Steinwerk Andelsbuch (gravel and stone quarry). Exploring the theme of "cottage industries", we visited a special exhibition at the Heimatmuseum and Angelika-Kaufmann-Museum in Schwarzenberg. Architect and curator Cornelia Faisst guided us around the show *Massai Women Master Builders from Ololosokwan* at the Frauenmuseum Hittisau— an unexpected and inspiring encounter with African architecture at the heart of the Alps! The Georunde Riedberg and "Felber's Schiefes Haus" in Sibratsgfäll brought to life the natural disaster of a landslide in 1999, impressively recounted by the former Mayor Konrad Stadelmann. The current Vice-Mayor and forester Christian Natter demonstrated how the forest is changing and what measures are being taken to adapt to climate change in Vorderwald-Egg as a model region. Together with the young Gault Millau-rated chef Milena Broger, the participants prepared an evening meal from waste vegetables in the "Gute Stube", a temporary-use project of the Offene Jugendarbeit Bregenzerwald headed by Agnes Hollenstein and assisted by Simone Angerer. Thanks to all craftswomen and craftsmen and people of Bregenzerwald!

It is, however, the students of *Design Investigations* at the University of Applied Arts Vienna who played the most important role with regard to the content and realisation of *After Abundance.* Taking up the challenging invitation with great professionalism, much sweat and application, they developed what was one of the most noted contributions to the London Design Biennale 2018. Great praise and respect are due for the educational instructions of the *Design Investigations* team—Orna Baumgartner, Nikolas Heep, Peter Knobloch, Justin Pickard, Bernhard Ranner and Stefan Zinell—and the many guest lecturers without whose participation and support the project would not have been possible to this level of quality. Realisation of the complex structure and the demanding set-up and strike in the rooms of Somerset House, that require special attention in terms of conservation, were in the capable hands of Professor Matthias Pfeffer. Special thanks are due to the Rector Dr. Gerald Bast as a reliable, supportive and critical partner. In the University's

150th year, he has once again demonstrated the pioneering international role of the Angewandte, and the publication on the Biennale entry is thanks to his commitment!

In the expert hands of Angelika Fössl from Birkhäuser Verlag and Anja Seipenbusch-Hufschmied, who is in charge of the Edition Angewandte, the documentation of the Biennale entry evolved into a specialist publication that showcases the interdisciplinary teaching and working method of *Design Investigations* for the first time. Here, sincere thanks are due also to the external authors and scientists from the field of climate research, the two professors Dr. Helga Kromp-Kolb and Dr. Kate Marvel. Aline Lara Rezende and Jennifer Cornick have revisited and summed up the speculative design projects and their authors objectively for this publication. We would like to thank Anindita Basu Sempere whose writing workshop helped the students articulate their projects into the written word.

The visual communication of the Biennale entry and the publication were excellently handled by Christof Nardin and Pascal Magino from Bueronardin. Publicising the Austrian entry to great effect in the country and abroad, the team at ABC Ana Berlin Communications proved equally capable. Personal thanks are due to Georg Geyer with his keen sense of art who provided us with help and advice throughout.

Coordinating and organising such a complex project with so many people involved is a feat that can only be accomplished with professionals. Equipped with their tremendous experience in overseeing various biennials, the team at section.a equally succeeded in bringing Austria's entry for London, *After Abundance,* to perfection. We would like to extend our special thanks to our associates Katharina Boesch and Viktoria Pontoni. Thanks to their structured approach, great calm and advice, the joy in being part of this project lasted up the last minute, and beyond!

Thomas Geisler, Anab Jain

DANK

Der Österreich-Beitrag *After Abundance* zur London Design Biennale 2018 ist ein Gemeinschaftsprojekt vieler Beteiligter. Der Weitsicht des Bundeskanzleramts ist es zu verdanken, dass die Bedeutung und Wichtigkeit einer Teilnahme Österreichs an dieser internationalen Ausstellung für zeitgenössisches Design erkannt wurde. Dem Bundesminister Gernot Blümel und der Sektion II für Kunst und Kultur im Bundeskanzleramt, vertreten durch Sektionschef Jürgen Meindl, sowie Gudrun Schreiber, Olga Okunev und Gerhard Jagersberger, möchten wir unseren besonderen Dank für das Vertrauen ausdrücken, den Biennale-Beitrag gestalten zu dürfen.

Die wiederholte Einladung Österreichs zur London Design Biennale zeigt die Wertschätzung und die internationale Anerkennung der kreativen Leistungen aus diesem Land. Der Biennale-Präsident Sir John Sorrel und der künstlerische Direktor Dr. Christopher Turner sowie das gesamte Team rund um Sumi Ghose waren nicht nur begeistert von *After Abundance,* sondern waren auch Ermöglicher*innen einer komplexen, raumgreifenden Installation in den historischen Räumlichkeiten des Somerset House. Wir möchten uns auch bei mischer'traxler studio (Katharina Mischer und Thomas Traxler), den Designer*innen des Biennale-Beitrags 2016, für die Beratung in der Anfangsphase der Ausstellungsentwicklung bedanken.

Für die Unterstützung vor Ort waren die Österreichische Botschaft unter der Leitung von Botschafter Dr. Michael Zimmermann und das Österreichische Kulturforum London unter der Leitung von Katalin-Tünde Huber mit ihren Mitarbeiter*innen Elisabeth Freudensprung, Christa Marchardt, Petra Freimund, Vanessa Fewster, Claudia Ott und Balachandra Arunachalam wichtige Partner*innen und Bindeglied zur Biennale.

Das Projekt erhielt zudem substanzielle Unterstützung aus den Bundesländern Vorarlberg und Wien. Ein besonderer Dank gilt der Abteilung Kultur des Landes Vorarlberg unter der Leitung von Landesrat Dr. Christian Bernhard und dem Abteilungsvorstand Dr. Winfried Nußbaummüller und ihrem Team in Bregenz. Dank der Vorarlberg Tourismus GmbH unter der Leitung von Christian Schützinger und der Betreuung von Gerald März und ihrem Team in Dornbirn, konnte gemeinsam mit der Österreich Werbung in London eine spezielle Informationsveranstaltung für internationale Medien ermöglicht und durchgeführt werden. Ein Dank gilt ebenso dem Unternehmen Bohlinger + Grohmann, das uns

mit seiner Expertise im Bereich der Statik unterstützt und wesentlich zur Umsetzung beigetragen hat.

Besondere Aufmerksamkeit erzielten – und in bester Erinnerung blieb – das von departure, dem Kreativzentrum der Wirtschaftsagentur Wien, unter der Leitung von Elisabeth Noever-Ginthör und der Betreuung von Alice Jacubasch und Ute Stadlbauer veranstaltete Eröffnungsfest für das Österreich-Team sowie die offiziellen Gäste und alle neu gewonnenen Freund*innen der Biennale. Österreich hat mit dem Fest einmal mehr seine Gastfreundschaft unter Beweis gestellt!

Eine Exkursion in den Bregenzerwald zum Projektstart ermöglichte Einblicke in das Leben und Arbeiten im ländlich-alpinen Raum sowie in die Herausforderungen und Anpassungen zum Klimawandel in der Region und global. Dazu zählte die Besichtigung von Handwerksbetrieben des Werkraum Bregenzerwald, insbesondere der Tischlerei Mohr, des Kies- und Steinwerks Andelsbuch. Zum Thema „Heimarbeit" besuchten wir eine Sonderausstellung im Heimatmuseum und Angelika-Kaufmann-Museum in Schwarzenberg. Die Architektin und Kuratorin Cornelia Faisst führte uns durch die Ausstellung *Maasai Baumeisterinnen aus Ololosokwan* im Frauenmuseum Hittisau – ein unerwartete und bereichernde Begegnung mit der Baukultur Afrikas mitten in den Alpen! Die Georunde Riedberg mit „Felber's Schiefem Haus" in Siebratsgfäll vergegenwärtige die Naturkatastrophe eines Hangrutsches von 1999, eindrücklich vermittelt vom ehemaligen Bürgermeister Konrad Stadelmann. Der jetzige Vizebürgermeister und Förster Christian Natter zeigte, wie sich der Waldbestand verändert und welche Klimawandel-Anpassungsmaßnahmen in der Region Vorderwald-Egg als Modellregion getroffen werden. Gemeinsam mit der jungen Haubenköchin Milena Broger wurde in der „Guten Stube", einem Zwischennutzungsprojekt der Offenen Jugendarbeit Bregenzerwald, ein Abendmenü aus Gemüseabfällen zubereitet. Allen beteiligten Handwerker*innen und Bregenzerwälder*innen sei Dank!

Den wesentlichsten Anteil am Inhalt und der Umsetzung von *After Abundance* tragen jedoch die Studierenden von *Design Investigations* an der Universität für angewandte Kunst in Wien. Sie haben die herausfordernde Einladung mit hoher Professionalität, viel Schweiß und Fleiß zu einem der meist beachteten Beiträge der London Design Biennale 2018 geführt. Großes Lob und Respekt gebührt der fachlichen und pädagogischen Anleitung durch das Team – Orna Baumgartner, Nikolas Heep, Peter Knobloch, Justin Pickard, Bernhard

Ranner und Stefan Zinell – sowie den vielen Gastvortragenden, ohne deren Mitwirkung und Unterstützung das Projekt nicht diese hohe Qualität hätte erreichen können. Die Realisierung der komplexen Konstruktion und der anspruchsvolle Auf- und Abbau in den konservatorisch heiklen Räumen des Somerset House waren bei Professor Matthias Pfeffer in den besten Händen. Ein besonderer Dank gilt Rektor Dr. Gerald Bast als verlässlichem Partner, Förderer und kritischem Gegenüber. Im 150. Jahr des Bestehens hat er einmal mehr die internationale Vorreiterrolle der Angewandten unter Beweis gestellt – die Publikation zum Biennale-Beitrag ist seinem Engagement zu verdanken!

In den profunden Händen von Angelika Fössl vom Birkhäuser Verlag und Anja Seipenbusch-Hufschmied, die die Edition Angewandte verantwortet, entwickelte sich die Dokumentation des Biennale-Beitrags zu einer fachlichen Publikation, die erstmals die interdisziplinäre Lehr- und Arbeitsmethode von *Design Investigations* vorstellt. Hier gebührt auch den externen Autorinnen und Wissenschaftlerinnen aus dem Feld der Klimaforschung, den beiden Professorinnen Dr. Helga Kromp-Kolb und Dr. Kate Marvel, ein herzliches Dankeschön. Aline Lara Rezende und Jennifer Cornick haben die spekulativen Designprojekte und ihre Autor*innen für diese Publikation nochmals aufgesucht und auf den Punkt gebracht. Wir möchten uns bei Anindita Basu Sempere bedanken, deren Schreibworkshop den Studierenden half, ihre Projekte in das geschriebene Wort zu bringen.

Die visuelle Kommunikation des Biennale-Beitrags wie auch der Publikation lag bei Christof Nardin und Pascal Magino von Bueronardin in den besten Händen. Eben dort wähnten wir uns auch beim Team von ABC Ana Berlin Communications – das den Österreich-Beitrag im In- und Ausland bestens publik machte. Ein persönlicher Dank gilt Georg Geyer, der uns als kunstsinniger Berater mit Rat und Tat zur Seite stand.

Ein solch vielschichtiges Projekt mit so vielen Beteiligten zu koordinieren und zu organisieren, gelingt nur mit Profis! Das Team von section.a hat durch seine große Erfahrung in der Betreuung verschiedener Biennalen auch Österreichs London-Beitrag *After Abundance* zur Perfektion gebracht. Ganz besonders möchten wir uns bei unseren Mitstreiterinnen Katharina Boesch und Viktoria Pontoni bedanken, durch deren Strukturiertheit, Ruhe und Beratung die Freude am Projekt bis zur letzten Minute und darüber hinaus anhält!

Thomas Geisler, Anab Jain

TEAM

CREDITS

CURATOR
Thomas Geisler

Bueronardin
S. 24

DESIGN INVESTIGATIONS LEAD
Anab Jain

Damian Griffiths
S. 43–44, 46–47, 49–52, 57, 58, 60–63,
65–68, 73, 75–82, 84, 89–90, 92–93, 95–100,
105–106, 108–110, 112–116

DESIGN INVESTIGATIONS TEAM
Stefan Zinell, Nikolas Heep, Matthias Pfeffer,
Peter Knobloch, Bernhard Ranner, Justin Pickard

Nikolas Heep, Mia Kim
S. 37

CORN CARTEL
Sarah Franzl, Bernhard Poppe, Julia Brandl,
Isabel Prade

Werner Heiss
S. 12

ILLEGAL RAIN
Florian Semlitsch, Lucy Li, Agnieszka Zagraba

Dennis Meadows et al. 1972
S. 24

RESTITUTION OF A GLACIER
Felix Lenz, Sophie Falkeis, Carmen Farr,
Ula Reutina

Justin Pickard
S. 18, 32, 33

THE HEISCHE
Fabio Hofer, Ali Kerem Atalay, Catherine Hu,
Catalina Gomez Alvarez

University of Applied Arts Vienna
S. 38, 54, 56, 69, 70, 72, 74, 85–86, 88, 101–104,
118–120, 122

MICROGRID
Mia Meusburger, Maximilian Scheidl, Silvio
Skarwan, Simon Platzgummer, Lisi Sharp

DWELLINGS FOR CHANGED
LIFESTYLES (Research)
Ege Kökel, Anna Neumerkel, Laura Hoek,
Lang Fei

IMPRINT

This publication was published on the occasion of the contribution to the London Design Biennale 2018.

London Design Biennale, *Emotional States,* Sept 4—23, 2018 Somerset House London, Strand, London WC2R 1LA, UK www.londondesignbiennale.com

After Abundance an installation of Design Investigations led by Anab Jain, curated by Thomas Geisler

After Abundance is a cooperative venture between the Werkraum Bregenzerwald and the Vienna University of Applied Arts, commissioned by the Austrian Federal Chancellery / Section II—Art and Culture.

EDITORS
Thomas Geisler, Werkraum Bregenzerwald, Andelsbuch, Austria
Anab Jain, Design Investigations (Industrial Design 2), Institute of Design, University of Applied Arts Vienna, Austria

TEXTS
Gerald Bast, Gernot Blümel, Thomas Geisler, Nikolas Heep, Anab Jain, Helga Kromp-Kolb, Kate Marvel, Justin Pickard, Aline Lara Rezende, Stefan Zinell

Library of Congress Control Number: 2018962435

Bibliographic information published by the German National Library The German National Library lists this publication in the Deutsche Nationalbibliografie; detailed bibliographic data are available on the Internet at http://dnb.dnb.de.

EDITING
Viktoria Pontoni, section.a

GRAPHIC DESIGN
Bueronardin

TRANSLATION
Richard Watts

PROOFREADING
Jennifer Cornick (English)
Claudia Mazanek (German)

PAPER
Fedrigoni Arcoprint Milk White
Gardapat 13 Kiara

COVER IMAGE
Bueronardin, after an idea by Fabio Hofer, Ali Kerem Atalay, Catherine Hu, Catalina Gomez Alvarez, Stefan Zinell, Nikolas Heep

REPROGRAPHICS
Bueronardin

PRINTING
Holzhausen Druck GmbH, Wolkersdorf, Austria

Project Management "Edition Angewandte" on behalf of the University of Applied Arts Vienna: Anja Seipenbusch-Hufschmied Project and Production Editor on behalf of the publisher: Angela Fössl

© 2019 Birkhäuser Verlag GmbH, Basel Postfach 44, 4009 Basel, Schweiz Part of Walter de Gruyter GmbH, Berlin/Boston

This book is also available as an E-Book (ISBN PDF 978-3-0356-1888-4)

ISSN 1866-248X
ISBN 978-3-0356-1860-0
www.birkhauser.com

PARTNER

dɪːˈʌngewʌndtə

vienna business agency
A service offered by the City of Vienna

G/G GEYER & GEYER
Steuerberatung

austrian cultural forum lon

VOR
ARL
BERG

BOLLINGER + GROHMANN
Ingenieure

ON BEHALF OF

 Bundeskanzleramt